GREAT IRISH PILGRIM JOURNEYS

Published by

CURRACHBOOKS
Block 3b, Bracken Business Park, Bracken Road
Sandyford, Dublin 18.
www.currachbooks.com

Copyright © 2025 John G. O'Dwyer

All rights reserved. Without limiting the rights under
copyright reserved alone, no part of this publication may be
reproduced, stored in or introduced into a retrieval system,
or transmitted, in any form or by any means (electronic,
mechanical, photocopying, recording or otherwise) without
the prior written permission of both the copyright owner and
the above publisher of the book.

First edition published in 2025

ISBN: 978-1-78218-937-4

Set in Adelle Font Family
Cover and book design by Alba Esteban
Layout by Pen Graphic Design
Printing: L&C, Poland

Pictures by the author John G. O'Dwyer unless stated otherwise

GREAT IRISH PILGRIM JOURNEYS

John G. O'Dwyer

CURRACH
BOOKS

Walking in the Irish outdoors can have an element of risk attached. The author and the publisher accept no responsibility for any injury, loss or inconvenience sustained by anyone while using this guidebook.

◄ Cosán na Naomh

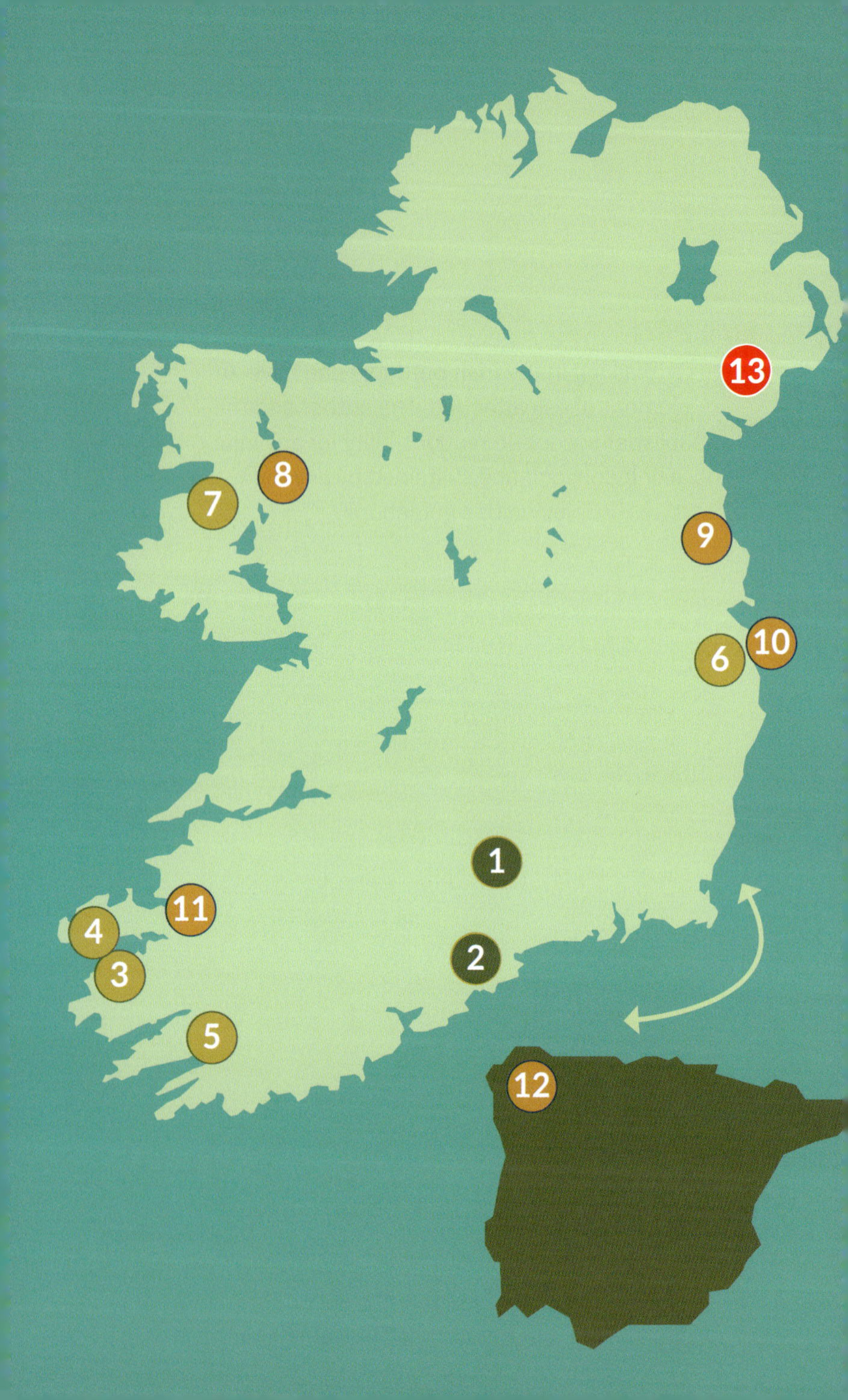
13
8
7
9
10
6
1
11
4
2
3
5
12

CONTENTS

INTRODUCTION 11

WALKING TIMES 17

ST DECLAN'S WAY

Introduction	21
1. St Declan's Way North	26
Day 1: Cashel to Cahir	29
Day 2: Cahir to Liam Lynch Trailhead	32
Day 3: Liam Lynch Trailhead to Mt Melleray	36
2. St Declan's Way South	40
Day 4: Mt Melleray to Cappoquin	42
Day 5: Cappoquin to Goish	45
Day 6: Goish to Ardmore	47

THE PILGRIM PASSPORT JOURNEY

Introduction	53
3. Cnoc na dTobar	54
4. Cosán na Naomh	62
5. St Finbarr's Pilgrim Path	72
Day 1: Drimoleague to Kealkill	74
Day 2: Kealkill to Gougane Barra	80
6. St Kevin's Way Wicklow	86
Day 1: Hollywood to Glendalough	86
Day 2: Alternative route from Valleymount	94
7. Tóchar Phádraig Mayo	96

THE CELTIC CAMINO

Introduction	108
8. Croagh Patrick Heritage Trail	112
Day 1: Balla to Ballintubber	116
Day 2: Ballintubber to Aughagower	118
Day 3: Aughagower to Murrisk	120
9. Boyne Valley Camino	122
10. Bray Coastal Camino	128

11. Kerry Camino	134
Day 1: Tralee to Camp	136
Day 2: Camp to Annascaul	138
Day 3: Annascaul to Dingle	141
12. A Coruna to Santiago	143
Day 1: A Coruna to Sergude	144
Day 2: Sergude to Hospital de Bruma	146
Day 3: Hospital de Bruma to Sigueiro	147
Day 4: Sigueiro to Santiago	149

ST PATRICK'S WAY

13. Introduction	152
Day 1: Navan Fort to Armagh City	156
Day 2: Armagh City to Tandragee	158
Day 3: Tandragee to Newry	158
Day 4: Newry to Rostrevor	160
Day 5: Rostrevor to Spelga Pass	161
Day 6: Spelga Pass to Newcastle	162
Day 7: Newcastle to Ballykinler	162
Day 8: Ballykinler to Downpatrick	165

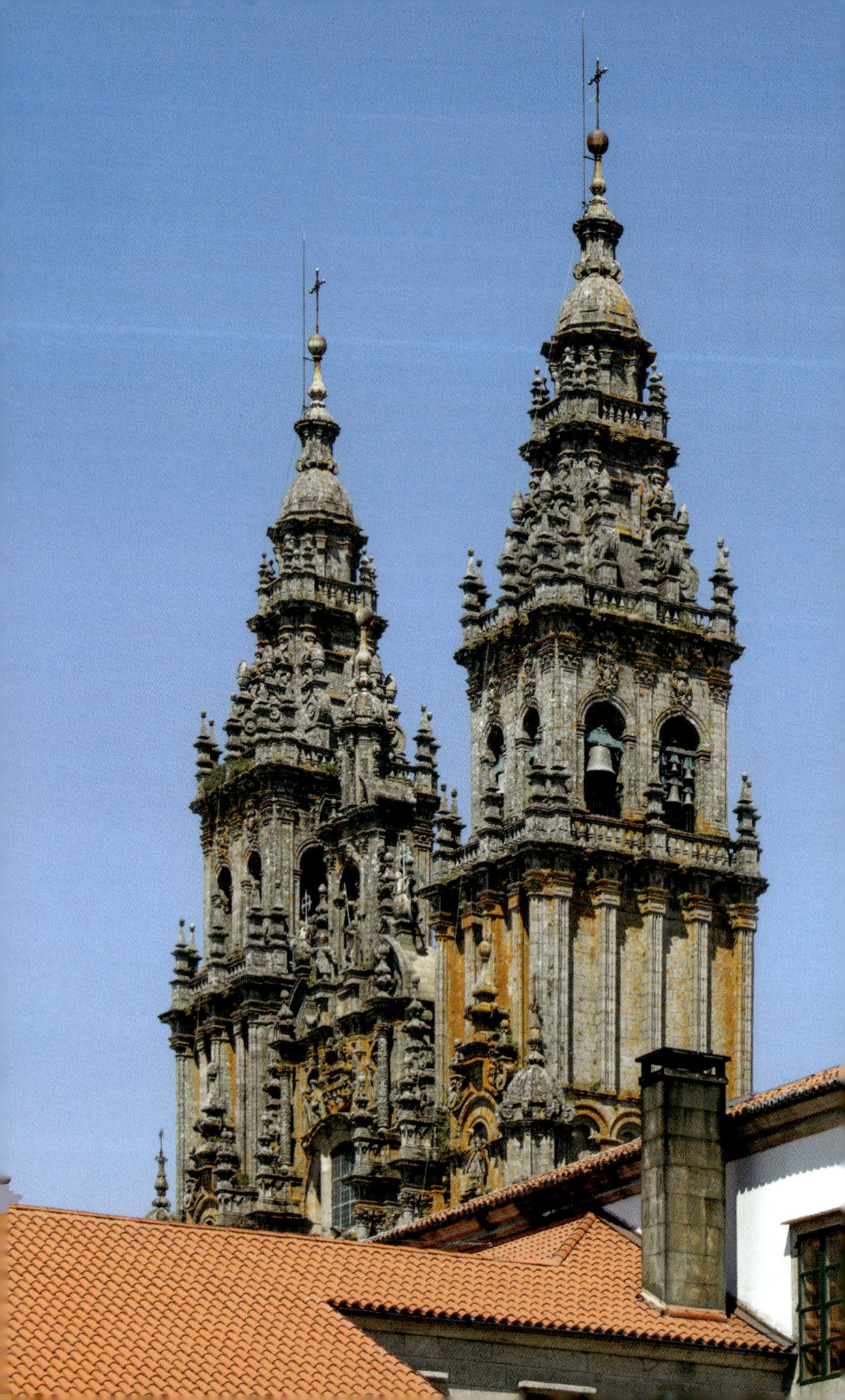

INTRODUCTION

In medieval times, pilgrimage involved a faith-based journey focused entirely on the destination. With those taking part having only a rudimentary knowledge of geography, the travelling was mostly regarded as a long, troublesome and often dangerous inconvenience leading to a meaningful conclusion. Having gained the holy site, it was believed that sanctity and healing would flow to those arriving with the right intentions and maybe with some money for offerings jangling in their pockets.

Many would have made the journey motivated by deep devotion to a saint venerated at the pilgrim site. Some would have come in a spirit of thanks for a favour bestowed, while others would have sought remission for their own sins or the sins of others in the form of indulgences, which offered a reduction of time spent suffering in purgatory. A smaller number would have been unwilling participants, ordered on pilgrimage as a penance to atone for their sins. Famously, Armagh man, Haneas MacNichaill was obliged to visit 19 places of pilgrimage in Ireland as a penance for murdering his son.

Medieval pilgrimage was an egalitarian endeavour, for it wasn't just the common people who undertook these arduous journeys into a scarily unknown world, for escaping hell fire proved a great medieval incentive for all. King Henry II of England undertook a redemptive journey to Canterbury in atonement for the murder of Archbishop Thomas Becket, while the Holy Roman Emperor, Henry IV, went barefoot in snow to beg Pope Gregory VII to

◄ Cathedral de Santiago de Compostela.
  Luis Miguel Bugallo Sánchez / Wikimedia

Cnoc na dTobar ▲

withdraw his excommunication. This meant he was no longer considered a member of the Christian Church, which might not seem a big problem for a ruler today and would probably elicit just a shrug of the shoulders. In those days, however, it was believed that, without forgiveness, excommunication from the Church condemned the individual to eternal damnation.

History is, of course, continually on the move and it was the Protestant Reformation splitting Christianity that ended the golden age of pilgrimage. A series of long-drawn-out sectarian wars were soon to virtually eliminate the trans-national spiritual journey, although some localised pilgrimage continued, mainly within the Catholic countries and generally outside the boundaries of the formalised Church.

But the basic human yearning to seek deeper meaning from a pilgrim journey could not be denied for long. Never an official part of Church doctrine, pilgrimage, nevertheless, resurrected itself during the 19th century in a democratic form of religious expression. Driven by a groundswell of demand from ordinary people in Catholic countries, and with the hierarchy often initially sceptical about apparitions, it manifested itself as an upsurge of travel to Marian shrines associated with the Blessed Virgin Mary, such as Lourdes, Knock and later Fatima.

These worshippers would mostly describe their journey as a pilgrimage, not to a site associated with an earlier saint but to a place where the Blessed Virgin is reputed to have manifested herself to mankind. Unlike medieval pilgrimage, where the tradition of walking arose from necessity, modern Marian pilgrims tend to be devout, Catholic and destination-focused; rarely if ever do they come on foot. Instead, these extremely fervent believers use trains, automobiles and planes to facilitate the journey.

More recently, the late 20th and early 21st centuries have been notable for another democratic movement that has arisen directly from the eternal human search for meaning. This involves looking back towards medieval times to heed the ageless siren call of the long walk to some mystical place of sanctity. For the individuals who undertake these journeys, the emphasis is, in the main, on simplicity, mindfulness and reflective experience with the path seen more as a voyage of inner discovery than as a physical challenge. Unlike Marian pilgrims, these individuals entirely forego mechanised transport to reach their destination and will most likely describe their journey, not as a pilgrimage but, as a pilgrim walk.

Most of these modern-day pilgrim walkers will choose to complete their path with friends or as part of an organised group. Some will decide to walk alone, but even for these individuals, there is a sense of belonging that is an inescapable part of the pilgrim endeavour. Others are likely to be encountered along the route by solo walkers with a sense of camaraderie, very often, developing rapidly with former strangers. But even when pilgrims sharing the route are not encountered, there is an echoing sense of walking in the footsteps of pilgrims past and experiencing a common purpose with them. It is this feeling of connection with others, either past and present, that, above all else, distinguishes 21st century pilgrim walking from hiking and is at the very foundation of penitential walking.

In contrast with those journeying to Marian shrines, large numbers of pilgrim walkers do not formally practice religion and so their journeys are not aimed at escaping hellfire or motivated by devotion to a saint. Instead, they are undertaken for more personal, holistic, cultural or wellness reasons with each person taking their own meaning from the experience.

St Augustine reputedly said, "Everything is solved by walking" and the journey more than the destination has now become the objective, with the sought-after personal renewal and self-discovery coming, not so much from the endpoint, as the walk itself. People now chase the elusive butterfly of fulfilment and self-awareness by heading for Iona in Scotland, Canterbury in England, along the Via Francigena to Rome and, above all, the Way of St James to Santiago de Compostela.

The Spanish Camino has undoubtedly been the European tourism phenomenon of the 21st century. Seeking meaning beyond materialism and recourse, for a time, to freer and less controlled way of living, the numbers completing this mystical Spanish trail have risen from fewer than 100 in 1967 to almost 450,000 in 2023. A win-win for Spanish tourism, the Camino has attracted spending away from the overcrowded Costas while bringing low-impact tourism to the Spanish Northwest.

Until recently, few of the multitudes attracted by the allure of a pilgrim walk along the Spanish Camino or other European routes would have considered Ireland an alternate destination, mainly because this country was believed to lack penitential trails. On the contrary, Ireland has a network of mystical paths and a vibrant pilgrim tradition, with all major routes long predating the Camino, some by up to a thousand years.

Historically, pilgrimage was an important devotional

expression for Irish people with penitents journeying to Glendalough, Gougane Barra, Croagh Patrick, Mount Brandon and Lough Derg. Later, during the 19th and 20th centuries, when an emphasis was placed on formal in-church worship, interest in the Irish pilgrim paths quickly evaporated and they became overgrown and largely forgotten.

It is sometimes said that the past, never completely dies but eventually, like Banquo's Ghost, comes to revisit us. And so it is that Irish history has come a full circle; people are again taking to these ancient tracks on about 400km of fully waymarked trails that follow the steps of penitents past. Pilgrimage these days is vastly different, with little overt emphasis on penance and prayer. Instead, people who follow the ancient spiritual trails of Ireland are generally a more casual and light-hearted bunch.

Coming in brightly coloured and stylish walk-wear, they generally don't seek a digital detox but carry their phones as they take on the challenges of completing a mystical walk. Some will stay in hostels or camp out, but for the majority,

View of Coragh Patrick from Aughagower

accommodation will be in comfortable hotels and B&Bs. Most have their backpack carried to the next destination, while none will take on the arduous task of footing it home, which medieval pilgrim walkers were obliged to accept. And unlike trail hikers who generally like to explore pristine environments with the minimum of past human influence, pilgrim walkers are happy to acquaint themselves with the well-trodden routes followed by past generations. And even the officially organised group walks are non-denominational and relaxed with more emphasis on history, mindfulness and engaging with the surroundings than on the prayerful origins of the route.

Nevertheless, pilgrim walking isn't just another form of hiking. As the modern expressions of spirituality become more informal and individual, pilgrimage has become as much a voyage of personal renewal as a physical journey. Materialism may squat immovably at the core of modern life, but the multitudes once again following the ancient tradition of a pilgrim walk are proof of a continuing desire for higher meaning that material wealth leaves unsatisfied.

Walking these paths allows each individual time to step away from the pressures of the 21st century. It provides an opportunity to slow down while reflecting on the purpose of life, with each participant taking a personal meaning from the route. Footing these ageless paths not only offers the opportunity for self-discovery, it also provides a link to the past while bringing welcome spending to Irish rural communities.

WALKING TIMES

Walking times in this book were calculated by hiking each route at a consistent but not particularly hurried pace and then recording only the time spent actually on the move. Obviously, walk durations will vary considerably with individual fitness and chosen pace, so the times quoted here should be treated as broad approximations only, with completion times often rising considerably in poor conditions.

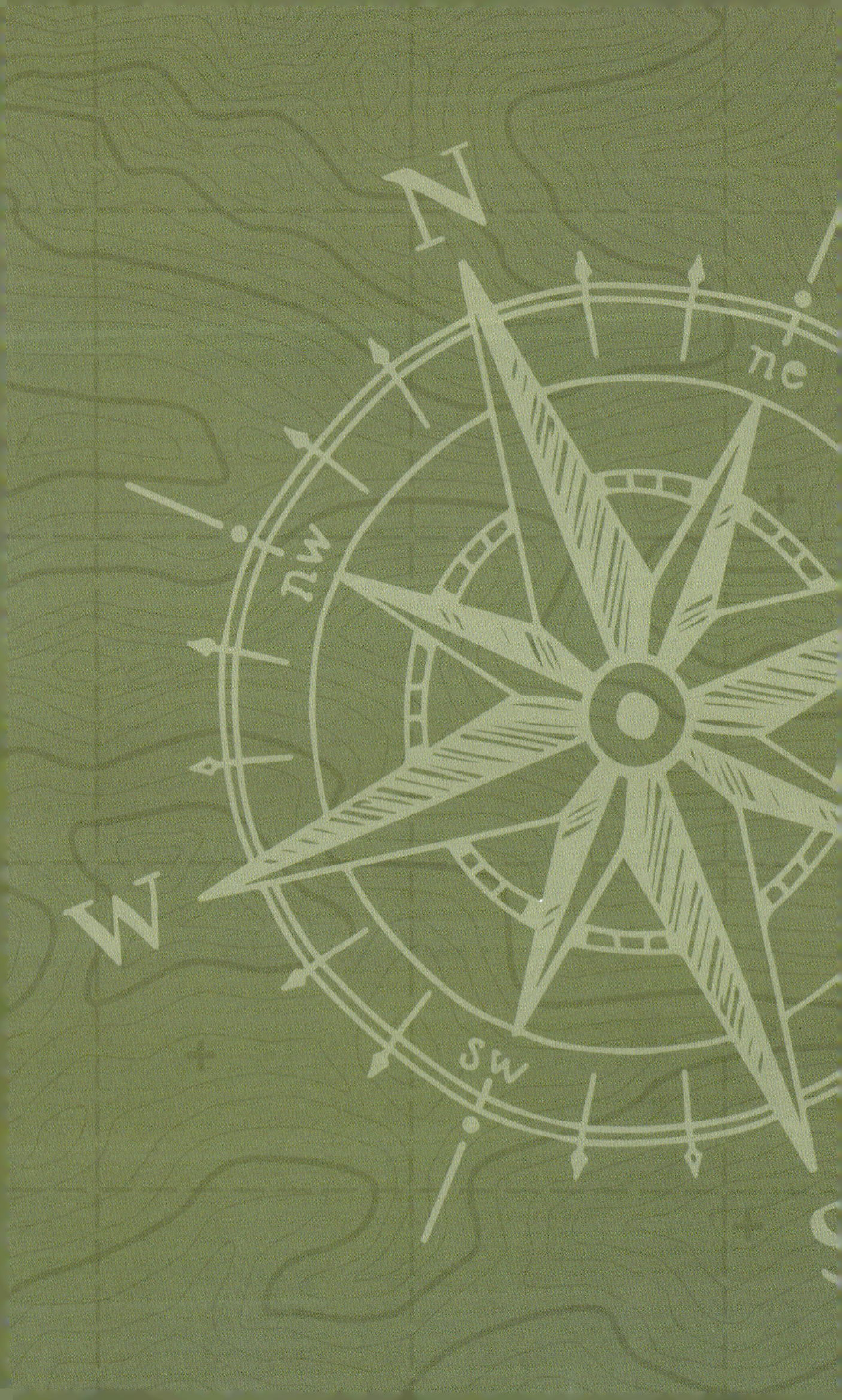
N
ne
nw
W
sw

ST·DECLAN'S WAY

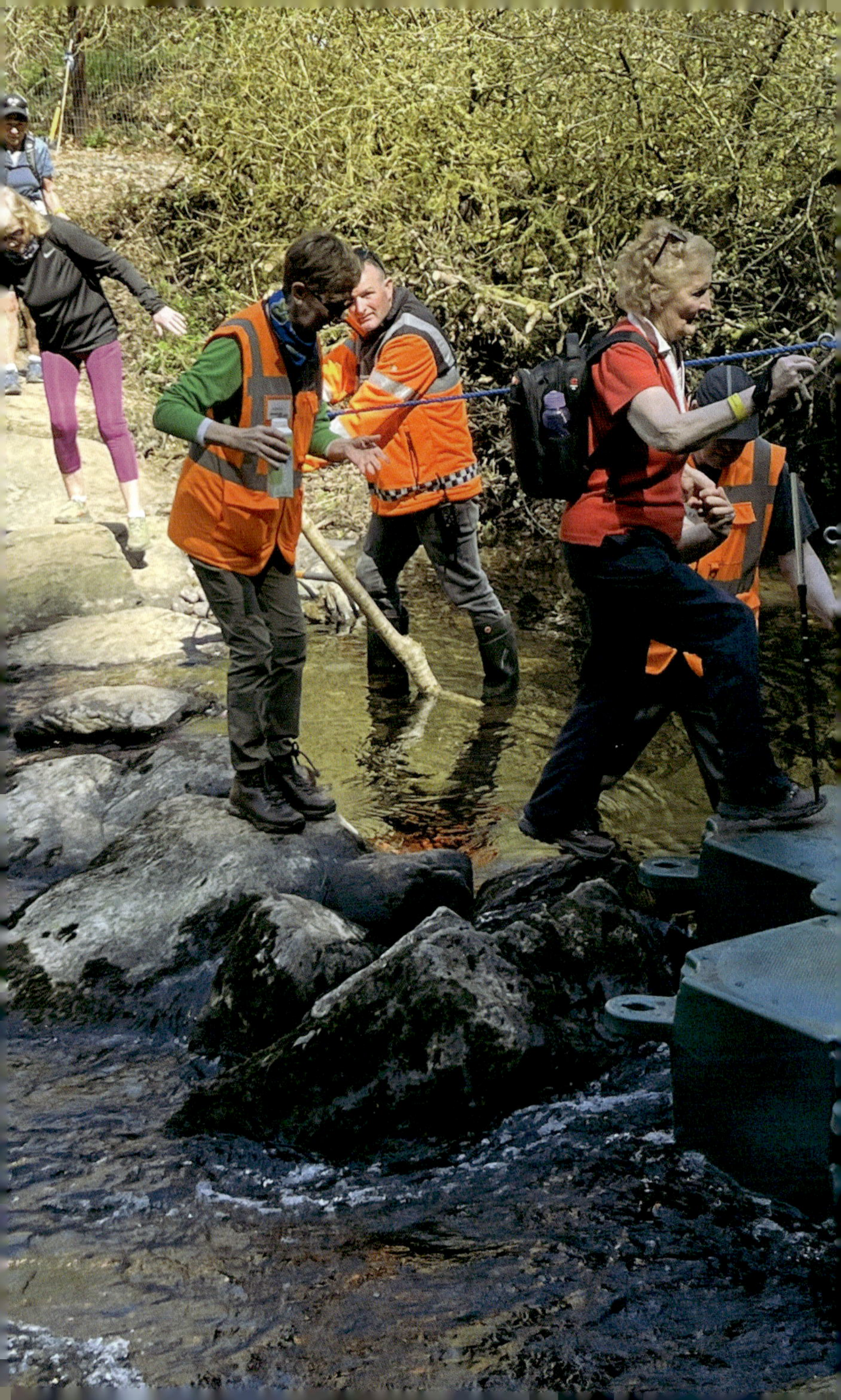

INTRODUCTION

Who was Ireland's first Christian missionary? The people of Ireland's southern Déise region will almost universally reply – and many historians will agree – that it was not Patrick, but Declan of Ardmore. Robust local belief holds Declan was born at Dromrue, near Cappoquin into a royal family in the Déise region, which extended over much the same area as the more modern diocese of Waterford and Lismore. After discovering about the coming of Christ and the new message of eternal life available to all, he journeyed in the early 5th century to study in the newly Christianised Roman Empire. Returning as a bishop, he began ministering in his native Déise.

Soon, however, he was disconcerted to hear accounts of a newly arrived, British-born evangelist, who was also preaching the gospel. Was he a true Christian and, if so, would he in some way disrupt Declan's ministry? To sort this out, legend has it that the southern saint travelled from Ardmore to royal Cashel, the traditional seat of the Munster Kings, and met with St Patrick.

Here, Declan discovered that Patrick was already one step ahead and had baptised Aenghus the King of Munster while carelessly impaling the royal foot with the point of his staff during the ceremony. Thinking it was all part of the ritual, Aenghus didn't complain and became Ireland's first Christian king.

It was now agreed by the two saints that Declan would have unchallenged authority over the Déise, with Patrick now declaring "Degláin, Pádraig na Déise" (Declan is the Patrick of the Déise). At the same time, Patrick would become Primate of all Ireland

Pilgrim walkers leaving the Rock of Cashel

– so face was saved on both sides. Wisely, the man who would later become known worldwide as Ireland's national apostle now refrained from crossing the mountain passes into the heart of the Déise on his missionary journey. This allowed Declan to remain supreme in his south Munster heartland, which he continues to do to this day, as the dominant and much-venerated saint of Co. Waterford.

History was then adroitly written to suit the needs of the time. To promote the interests of the Northern church, Patrick, the first Bishop of Armagh was exalted to superstar status as a saint. He was then promulgated above Declan of Ardmore as the first evangeliser to minister among the Irish people. Despite his ensuing obscurity, a robust tradition reaches down through the centuries that refers to Waterford's patron saint Christianising much of the south and making many journeys by chariot from Ardmore to the royal seat at Cashel.

And Declan's memory was not forgotten. The 115km trail

was, for countless generations, walked by pilgrims following the presumed journey taken by Declan on his way to and from Cashel. In more recent years the route fell into disuse but after a decade of urging from Ardfinnan man Kevin O'Donnell, the path was officially reopened in 2021. Leading pilgrims from the Rock of Cashel to the Celtic Sea, the route is now fully approved by Sport Ireland as a waymarked long-distance walking trail.

Developed with the cooperation of over 50 private landowners, Declan's Way incorporates several medieval pilgrimage routes such as the Rian Bó Phádraig, Bóthar na Naomh, Cosán na Naomh and St Declan's Road. This means Ireland now has a linear pilgrim trail that is comparable, in length and distance, with what most pilgrims undertake on the Spanish Camino.

Many hikers complete St Declan's Way in five days. For a rewarding experience, however, giving time to absorb the variety of landscapes and many antiquities en route, I would recommend a six-day outing. If you do it in 6 days, St Declan's Way breaks conveniently into 6 stages: 3 stages north of Melleray and 3 stages to the south.

OVERVIEW

A journey back in time of over 1,500 years, Ireland's answer to the Spanish Camino with the thermostat suitably turned down, breaks conveniently into six stages. With 3 stages north of Mount Melleray Abbey and 3 stages to the south, Declan's Way is perfect for a 6-day walking holiday in Ireland. These are now fully waymarked with the blue St Declan's Way arrows and the Slí Dhéagláin signposts at important junctions. Those wishing to have evidence of completing the entire pilgrim path can obtain a St Declan's Way Passport free of charge and stamp it at the designated points on the route.

Before setting out walkers should, however note, that, at the time of writing, on-route shopping facilities are only available

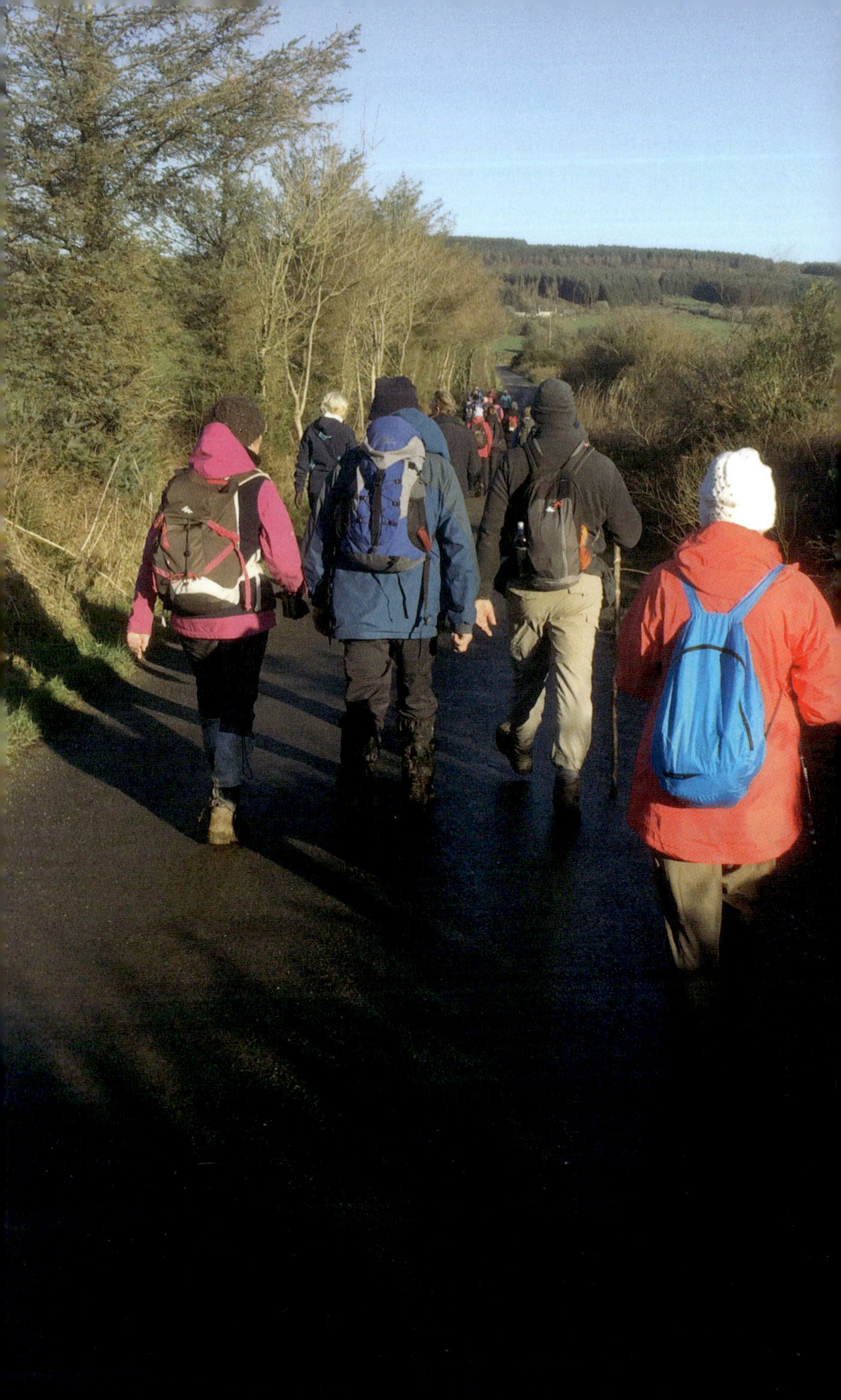

in Cashel, Cahir, Ardfinnan, Lismore, Cappoquin and Ardmore, so it is important to pack with this in mind. Accommodation may also be problematic to find, particularly around Aglish and Goatenbridge. You will, however, find an up-to-date listing of hospitality offerings nearby the route, the stamping points for the Passport along with other useful information by visiting www.stdeclansway.ie.

With regard to maps, sheets 66 and 74 of the Ordnance Survey Ireland, Discovery Series cover the first 4 stages of the route, while map sheets 74, 81 and 82, cover the last 3 stages. The path is densely waymarked, however, so maps should not be necessary.

Note: *the six stages described above are merely suggestions aimed at maintaining a relatively similar walking distance each day. Walkers can, of course, make other arrangements to suit their purposes.*

A tradition has also developed that the route is walked from north to south, that is from the Rock of Cashel to the Celtic Sea at Ardmore. The description below follows this orientation, which allows for a lovely coastal finish along the beach at Ardmore. This is not obligatory, however, as St Declan's Way is marked in both directions and some walkers have preferred to finish at Cashel.

01 ST DECLAN'S WAY NORTH CASHEL TO MOUNT MELLERAY

Suitability: *Ancient trail leading from Cashel, Co. Tipperary to Mount Melleray Abbey, Co. Waterford. Stages 1 and 2 are unchallenging with generally hill-free terrain that consists of quiet roads, riverside paths and some rustic lanes. Stage 3 is somewhat more challenging with a fairly continuous, but never over-demanding, ascent to the Liam Lynch Monument. Beyond, the trail levels for a while before rising to gain the Tipperary/Waterford border. After a short descent, it ascends again to reach the highest point of the route at 440m before sweeping down to a memorable woodland finish at Mount Melleray Abbey.*

Getting there: *Leave the M8 Motorway at junctions 7, 8 or 9 for Cashel. St Declan's Way begins from the carpark beneath the Rock of Cashel.*

Start: *Main Rock of Cashel carpark.*

Finish: *Mount Melleray Abbey.*

Estimated Time: *3 days.*

Distance: *59km.*

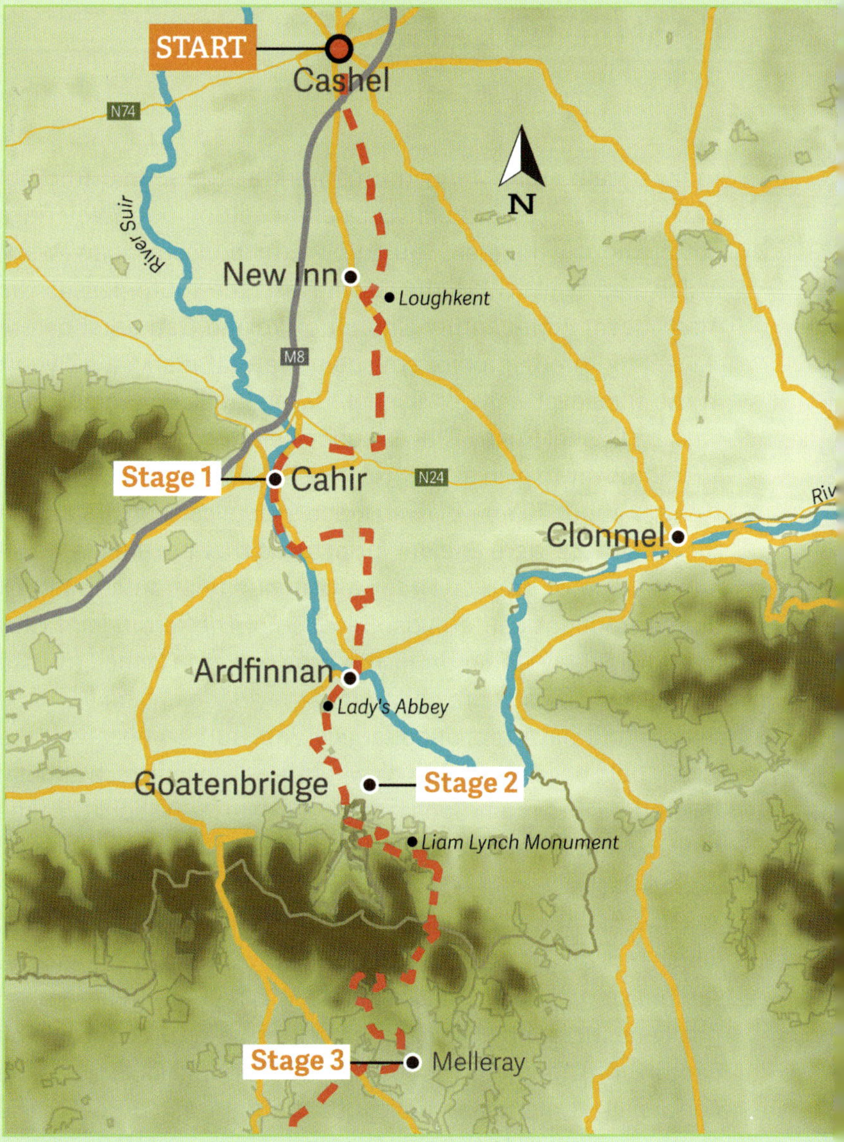

openstreetmap.org

DAY 1
CASHEL TO CAHIR
20KM

Today's walk starts from the carpark at the iconic Rock of Cashel, which you should visit before setting out if you have not previously done so. You go by a ruined Dominican Priory, which was built within the town. Next, the route passes the magnificent 18th-century Church of Ireland Cathedral before traversing through a modern sculpture that marks a sallyport in the medieval walls of Cashel. Beyond, follow a minor road passing Cashel Rugby Club grounds before crossing above the M8 motorway to gain a quiet rural road.

After about 700m, you will notice a large earthen ringfort on the left. These were ancient farmsteads that provided a home and a place of protection for a community and its livestock during frequent cattle raids. Because of the fertile land they are particularly common in the area around Cashel. In Irish mythology, ringforts are considered the abode of fairies or little people and have remained largely undisturbed because of a widely held belief that bad luck would befall anyone rash enough to interfere with them. Such farmsteads date from about the time of Declan and it may be that this one existed when the Saint visited Cashel.

Onwards now to the medieval era church ruins at Loughkent, which most likely was the site of an early Christian settlement. A monastery in the medieval period, it is reputed to have been finally destroyed by Oliver Cromwell as he returned from the capture of Clonmel in 1650. You will notice a bullaun stone containing a manmade hollow to the right as you enter the southern gateway to the site. The exact purpose of these stones is unclear, but they are most often found at shrines and places of pilgrimage and in Christian times may have been adopted for use as holy water fonts. In the 18th century, Loughkent became a burial place at a time when penal laws did not allow the new Catholic graveyards to be consecrated. Today, Loughkent is a serene place that makes for a perfect lunch stop.

Reinvigorated, continue through a pleasant farming landscape leading to the busy R687. Follow this road left for about 400m before escaping right along a lane that leads you through a farmyard. From here, the route continues south through the rolling Tipperary countryside before doglegging west with the mighty Galtee Mountains as a spectacular backdrop to reach historic Cahir. In the Irish language, the town is known as Cathair Dún Iascaigh (town of the fort of the fishery). It boasts many fine Georgian buildings including St Pauls Church of Ireland Cathedral, which you will pass by as you enter the town. Your walk ends in the carpark beside the great Norman Castle of the Butlers.

THE ROCK OF CASHEL

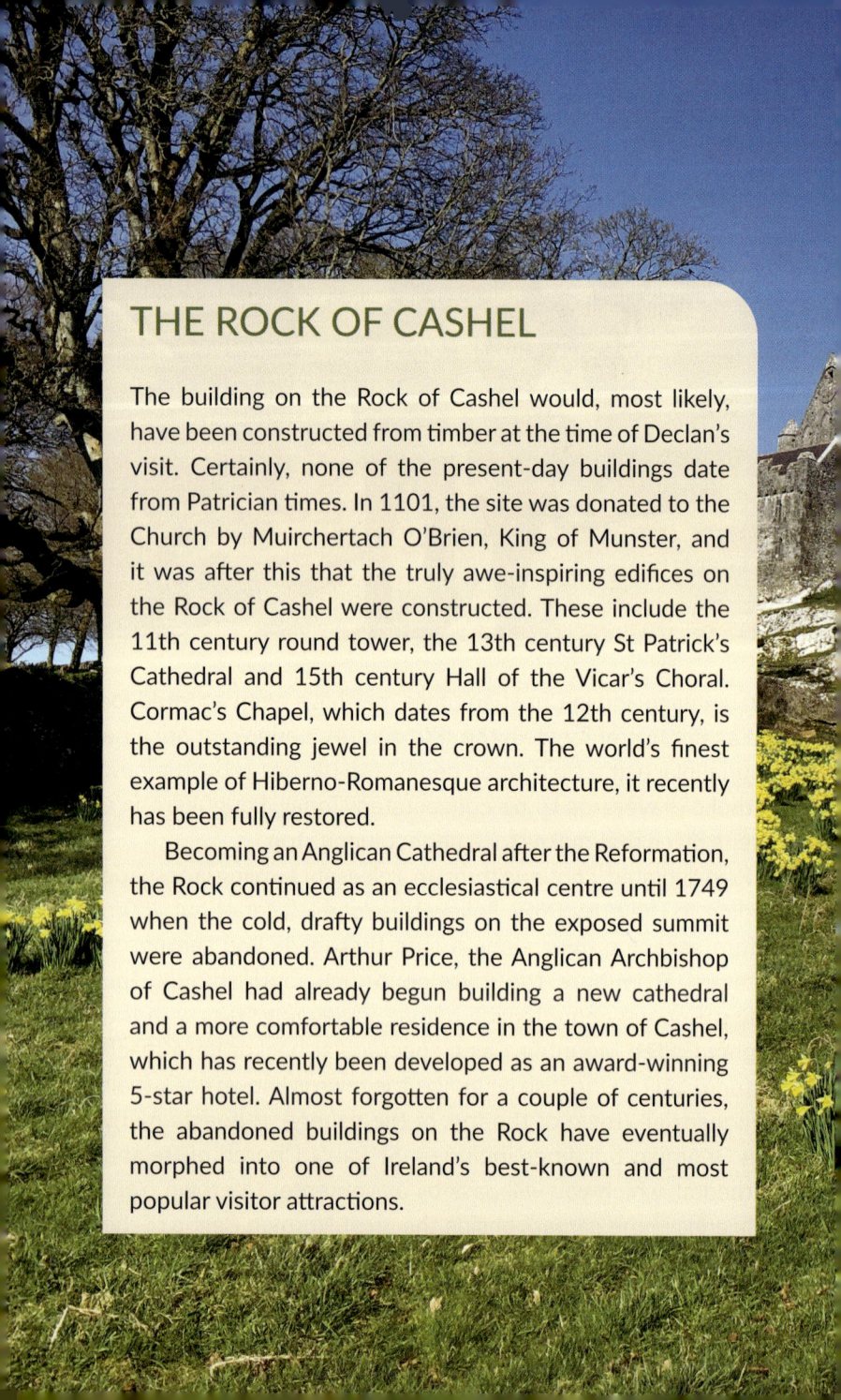

The building on the Rock of Cashel would, most likely, have been constructed from timber at the time of Declan's visit. Certainly, none of the present-day buildings date from Patrician times. In 1101, the site was donated to the Church by Muirchertach O'Brien, King of Munster, and it was after this that the truly awe-inspiring edifices on the Rock of Cashel were constructed. These include the 11th century round tower, the 13th century St Patrick's Cathedral and 15th century Hall of the Vicar's Choral. Cormac's Chapel, which dates from the 12th century, is the outstanding jewel in the crown. The world's finest example of Hiberno-Romanesque architecture, it recently has been fully restored.

Becoming an Anglican Cathedral after the Reformation, the Rock continued as an ecclesiastical centre until 1749 when the cold, drafty buildings on the exposed summit were abandoned. Arthur Price, the Anglican Archbishop of Cashel had already begun building a new cathedral and a more comfortable residence in the town of Cashel, which has recently been developed as an award-winning 5-star hotel. Almost forgotten for a couple of centuries, the abandoned buildings on the Rock have eventually morphed into one of Ireland's best-known and most popular visitor attractions.

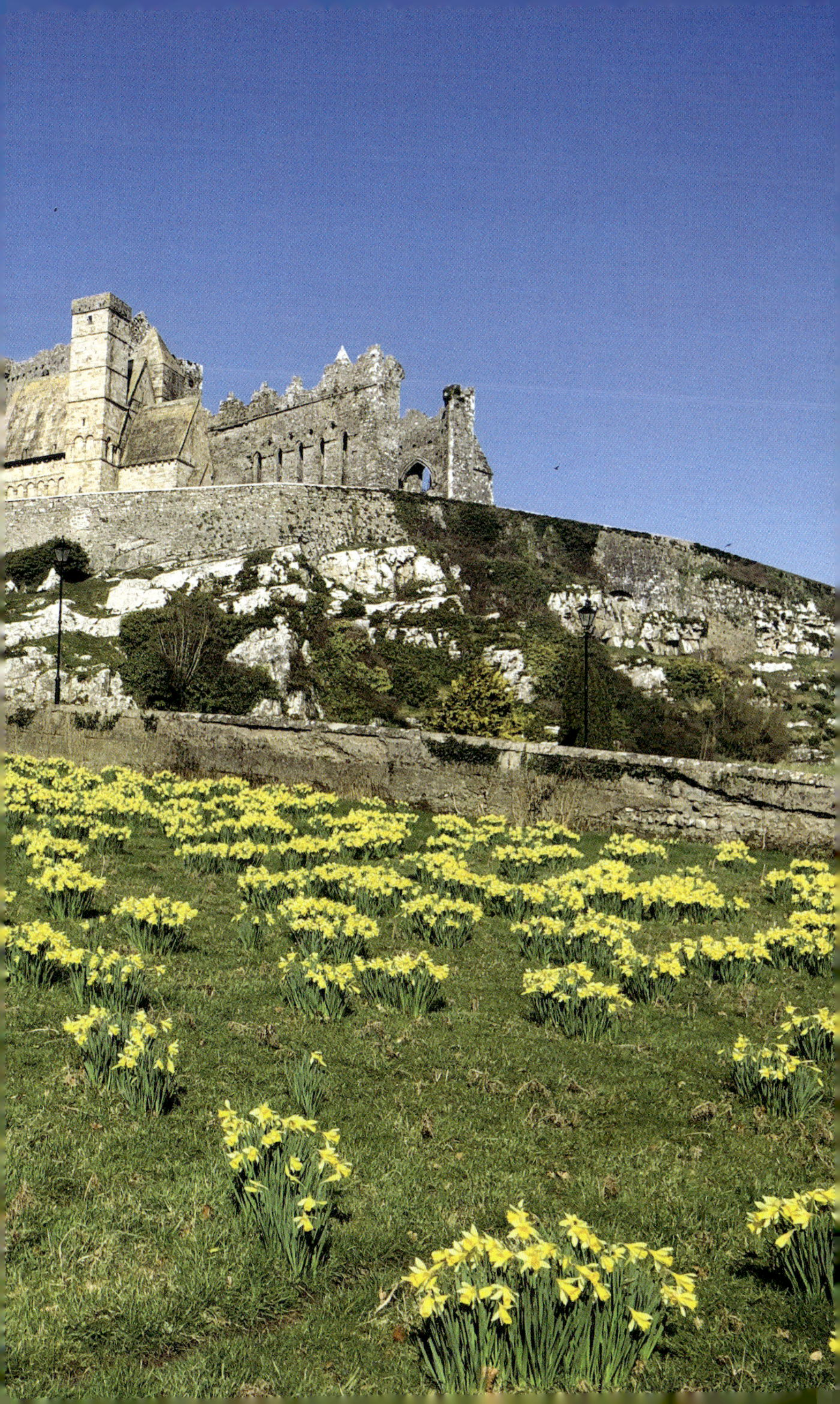

Knockmealdown Mountains from Goatenbridge

DAY 2
CAHIR TO LIAM LYNCH TRAILHEAD
20KM

It is a magnificent start today. Begin from beside the ramparts of the great Norman Castle that dominates the town and is well worth a pre-walk visit. Perched on a rocky island in the River Suir, Cahir Castle was built in the 13th century by the powerful Butler family of Ormond. Considered impregnable before the invention of gunpowder, it was eventually captured by the Earl of Essex in 1599 when heavy artillery was used to blast through its walls. Passing by the Castle, see if you can spot the canon ball from this period lodged in the outer wall of the Northeast Tower.

Continue by following the River Suir south along a sublime woodland pathway for about 1.5km to reach the ornamental iron bridge leading to the Swiss Cottage – a fine example of a 19th-century "cottage orné". Then, it is on by a riverside path that soon concedes to quiet byroads with grass down the centre. After a T-junction, the way is south with the magnificent Knockmealdown Mountains now filling the horizon until you cross Factory Hill and then sweep down to reach the picturesque village of Ardfinnan. On the way you will pass an Anglican Church which is reputed to have been built where a monastery on the site was established in the 7th century by St Finian Lobhar, who also founded a renowned monastery on Innisfallen Island in the Lakes of Killarney. Cross the bridge over the River Suir. This is located beneath a 12th-century Norman Castle, built by England's Prince John, which once guarded an important crossing point on the river. Since the village boasts shopping facilities and a small restaurant, this makes a good place to tarry for lunch on the picturesque and riverside village green.

Beyond Ardfinnan, are the remains of a 19th-century fever hospital on the right and soon after the ivy-covered ruins of the medieval Ladys Abbey. This was founded in the 14th century as a Carmelite Friary, but little else is known about its history.

Now the route begins descending gently with the great ramparts of the Knockmealdown Mountains towering ahead as a constant backdrop. You now swing right, left and then left again before another excursion along a rural laneway leads to the Tar River. This is crossed by a pretty footbridge leading to a laneway that is known locally as Bóthar Caoch (the Blind Road). Crossing the Clogheen to Newcastle main road at Kildanogue Cross, continue straight ahead on the tarmac before this segues to a gravel path. At the next T-Junction, go right before ending your day at the trailhead carpark for the Liam Lynch Loop.

THE SWISS COTTAGE

Located on a high point above the River Suir, the Swiss Cottage was built by Richard Butler, 1st Earl of Glengall in the early 19th century. It is based on a design by the renowned 19th-century English architect John Nash, who also drew the plans for Buckingham Palace. The Cottage is inspired by the idea of an idyllic rural lodge with its bucolic features including a distinctive thatched roof while its external woodwork resembles the branches of trees. The asymmetrical design of the cottage is deliberate; it is aimed to make it seem unsophisticated and natural. The nature theme continues throughout the internal furnishings and wallpaper. The cottage opens to the public seasonally, generally from April to October.

Photograph by Stefan Riesner / Wikimedia

DAY 3
LIAM LYNCH TRAILHEAD TO MOUNT MELLERAY ABBEY
19KM

Today encompasses one of the highlights of your walk: the crossing of the Knockmealdown Mountains. After a steady upward ascent of about 3.5km on benign forest roadways that are signposted for the Liam Lynch Monument, you reach a large round tower guarded by 4 bronze wolfhounds. This was constructed in 1935 to honour republican leader Liam Lynch, who was shot at this exact spot during the Irish Civil War, as he tried to escape from the army of the newly independent Irish Free State. This killing had the practical effect of ending the conflict.

An undemanding forest roadway, offering an expansive panorama to the left over the River Suir and Tar Valleys, now conveys you for about 1km to a turning circle. Here the way is upwards to the right on an informal trail through mountain scrubland, which probably has a strong resemblance to what medieval pilgrim tracks might have looked like. This soon gives way to an agricultural lane leading past small fields and a ruined dwelling. Next, it is right and over a metal stile to gain a green path serenely doglegging downhill to a tiny road. Now, the way is right and generally uphill towards a magnificent viewing point known locally as The Crois that marks your entry into Co. Waterford. Here stands the ruins of a 19th-century barracks that belonged to a pre-Irish Independence police force known as the Royal Irish Constabulary. It was abandoned during the Irish War of Independence.

Serene Glounafalla lies directly below, while the great expanse of the Waterford lowlands drifts away to the Blackwater Valley and the ocean beyond. Descending, you will soon reach Billy

Byrnes Bridge, which spans the Glenafallia River. Here, the path dives off-road to the right on a broad green path before going sharply right again. Here it rises steeply to gain open mountain on what you will probably find the steepest pull of the day. The route continues ascending to a point on the southern slopes of Knocknafallia, (The Hill of the Cliff) which, at 440m, marks the highest elevation on the entire trail. The route now rises and falls as it tracks a forest edge before crossing a tiny canal, laboriously dug by industrious Cistercian monks that draws water from a mountain stream. Known locally as 'The Source', it was built to provide Melleray with water supplies and acts as a reminder that, until the Industrial Revolution, most technological advances in Europe emerged from monasteries.

Soon after, the trail dives left into woodland at a gate and then meanders mostly downhill through the trees. Eventually, you pass an ornamental building housing the well, which supplied drinking water to Melleray. Beyond, is a reservoir, before the route crosses a short causeway and goes right again to tag arrows through farm buildings before finally gaining the renowned Cistercian Abbey. Here, a simple message carved in stone proclaims your present situation, *"I am a passing guest, a pilgrim, like those who went before me."* In November 2024, it was announced by the Cistercian Order that Mount Melleray Abbey was to close, as an interim measure, with the remaining monks and lay brothers transferring to Mount St Joseph's Abbey, Roscrea. With effect from January 26, 2025, the three Cistercian communities of Mount Melleray, Mellifont and Mount St Joseph merged as one community, based at Roscrea.

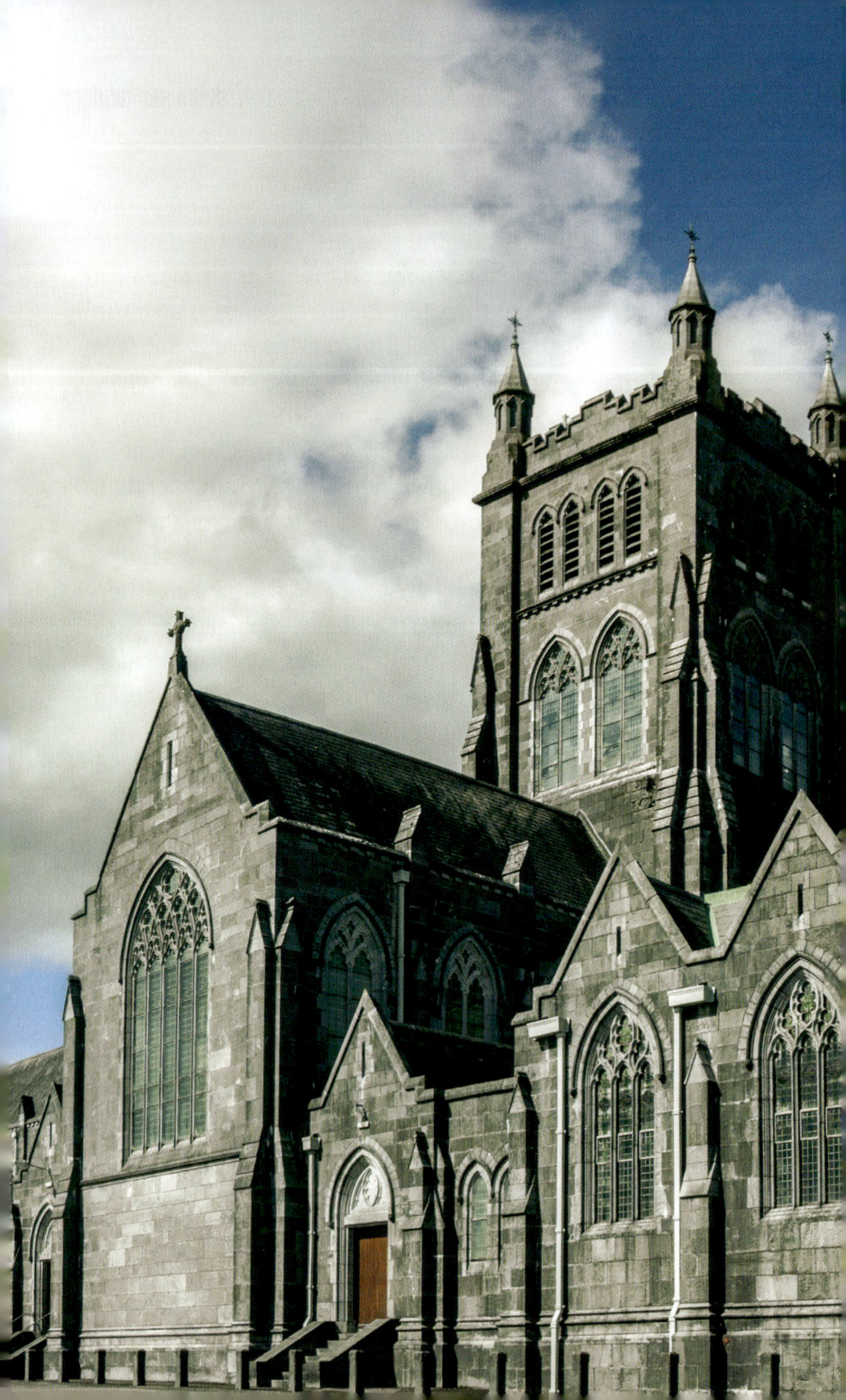

MOUNT MELLERAY ABBEY

The original Melleray Abbey was a Cistercian foundation located in Brittany until its monks were expelled from France following a wave of anticlericalism during the 2nd French Revolution of 1830. Taking advantage of a new religious tolerance of Catholicism in Ireland, they sailed to Cork under the leadership of Abbot Vincent Ryan and received a rapturous welcome as the first monastic order to have returned to Ireland since the reign of Henry VIII. Farming has traditionally been part of the Cistercian way of life but acquiring land proved to be a challenging problem.

Briefly settling at Rathmore, Co. Kerry, on land that soon proved unsuitable, the monks were then informed that a tract of mountainside was on offer at Srahan, Co. Waterford. Since this impoverished land was the best available, a price was agreed with the owner, Sir Richard Keane, who believed correctly that the Cistercians would draw additional business to the area in the form of visitors and agricultural produce. The local community in Co. Waterford then flocked to the monk's aid with thousands of men from the surrounding parishes coming to donate labour. Work went ahead quickly with the mountainside soon rendered fertile and productive. Six years after their arrival, the monastic church was consecrated. This was the first in Ireland since the dissolution of the monasteries during the English Reformation.

02 ST DECLAN'S WAY SOUTH MOUNT MELLERAY TO ARDMORE

Suitability: *Route leads to the ancient monastic site at Ardmore, Co. Waterford with only a few minor ascents involved. The terrain consists of woodland paths, quiet back roads and rustic lanes with a glorious finish along a sandy beach to Ardmore.*

Getting there: *St Declan's Way South begins from the village of Cappoquin, which is located on the N72 linking Dungarvan with Fermoy.*

Start: *Mount Melleray Abbey.*

Finish: *Ardmore monastic site.*

Estimated Time: *3 days.*

Distance: *56.5km.*

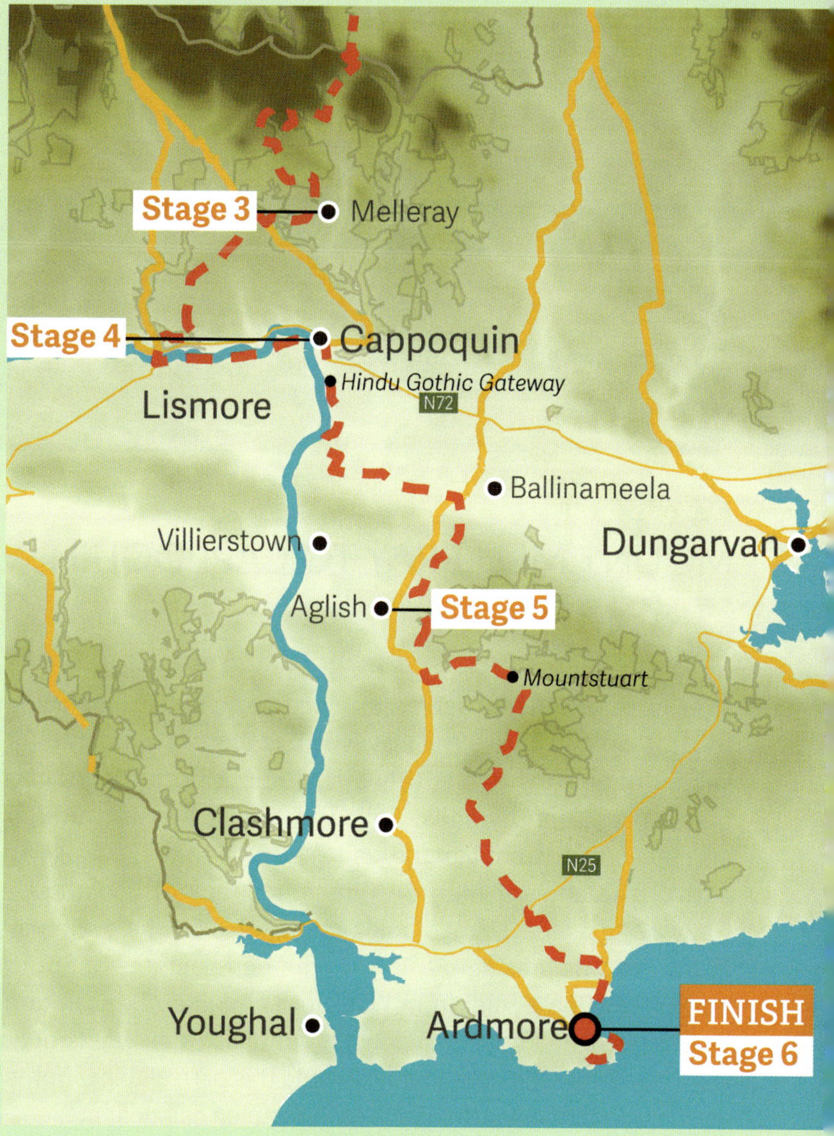

openstreetmap.org

Leaving Mount Melleray

DAY 4
MOUNT MELLERAY TO CAPPOQUIN
17.5KM

A traverse of the monastery farmlands by a rustic lane leads to a minor road where the way is left. Swing right for about a kilometre along the relatively busy R669, before turning left onto quiet, rural byroads. Follow the blue arrows through several junctions until an off-road excursion to the left follows part of the ancient Rian Bó Phádraig (Track of St Patrick's Cow) along a lane. Legend holds that a huge bovine owned by St Patrick was grazing placidly on the rich pastures of South Tipperary when a thief from Waterford abducted her calf and bore it over the Knockmealdown Mountains to his home near the River Bride. The cow angrily created this path with her horns as she thundered south to recover her stolen calf near present-day Lismore. Beyond the Rian, follow a quiet road offering an expansive view over the Blackwater Valley and Lismore for about a kilometre before diverting left by a farmyard.

A rural lane followed by an attractive woodland path leads to a road, along which you descend past Ballyrafter House to arrive at the R668. A further excursion by the banks of the Owennashade River then decants you to a magnificent bridge over the River Blackwater, offering superb views of Lismore Castle. Beyond the bridge, St Declan's Way bypasses Lismore, but the town makes an ideal place to stop for lunch and perhaps visit the Heritage Centre since you only have about 6km further to walk. Lismore was, in the early medieval period, a great centre of learning attracting students from all over Europe including the future king of the Anglo-Saxons, Alfred the Great. Afterward, leave the town by Lady Louisa's Walk: a lovely woodland path created by Lady Louisa Cavendish of Lismore Castle. For about 2km, the serene River Blackwater remains continually on your left until the route eventually joins a minor road. This conveys you to the elegant Avonmore Bridge, over the Blackwater and then into Cappoquin for your overnight stop.

Approaching Lismore

ST DECLAN'S WAY   43

LISMORE

Founded as a monastery in the 7th century by St Carthage, Lismore later became renowned as a seat of learning and is well worth taking an hour or two to explore, particularly the beautiful Church of Ireland Cathedral of St Carthage, which lies on the route of St Declan's Way. Above the town, tower the great ramparts of Lismore Castle. Built in 1185 by King Henry II to guard the river crossing, it was at one stage owned by favourite of Queen Elizabeth I, Sir Walter Raleigh. The castle is now the Irish seat of the English Dukes of Devonshire and was visited by future American President, John F Kennedy and Hollywood actor, Fred Astaire. It has magnificent gardens attached, that are open to the public. with an admission fee applying. The interior of the Castle is not accessible but can be viewed through the Lismore Castle virtual reality experience at the Heritage Centre, located in the town centre.

Photograph by Raúl Corral/ Wikimedia

DAY 5
CAPPOQUIN TO GOISH
18KM

Today, the route lies east of the mighty River Blackwater, which is navigable up to Cappoquin. In this area known as Affane, a great battle was fought in 1565 between 2 powerful Norman Irish families – the Butlers (Earls of Ormond) and the Geraldines (Earls of Desmond). This would be the last major battle fought in Ireland without foreign involvement. The Butlers emerged victorious with the result that the power of the Geraldines was forever broken in their South Munster heartland.

Next to capture your curiosity will undoubtedly be the spectacular Hindu Gothic Gateway and bridge over the River Finisk leading to Dromana House, which spans your route. Afterward, little frequented roads convey you eastwards past the ruins of Kilmolash Church. Dedicated to St Molaise – an obscure Irish saint from the early Christian era – the existent buildings all date from the later medieval period. Reaching Ballinameela, abandon the tarmac as the route swings abruptly south along the ancient tracks of the original pilgrim route, which provides a profound sense of walking into the past. Finally, you join a quiet back road leading to your destination for the day at the townland of Killatoor. Here a sign points 1.2km west across the R671 to Aglish village, where shopping facilities are available if required. The final stage of your pilgrimage leads south from Killatoor and follows rural boreens to Goish, which is just a 3-way crossroads that conveniently marks the end of your day's walk.

HINDU GOTHIC GATEWAY

The Hindu Gothic Gateway at Dromana was originally built as a temporary structure by local people to welcome the popular local lord, Francis Villiers Stuart, on his return from honeymoon. While staying in Brighton he had written home to extol the beauty of the Royal Pavilion built by King George IV as a magnificent oriental palace in a Hindu style. Francis liked his new Hindu Gothic entrance so much that he recreated it as a permanent structure and in this way gave employment locally during the Great Irish Famine of the 1840s.

Photograph by Madelien Knight/Wikimedia

DAY 6
GOISH TO ARDMORE
21KM

Beyond Goish, the way lies east through the pastoral countryside before swinging south at the entrance for St Patrick's Church at Mount Stuart. Notable for its woodland setting, this church was built before Catholic Emancipation in Ireland by Lord Henry Mount Stuart in 1826 for his Catholic tenants. Afterward, at a time when Catholics could not take a seat in Parliament, Daniel O'Connell asked Catholic voters to support Protestant candidates, who would give an undertaking that they would vote for Catholic Emancipation if elected. Henry Villiers Stuart became the first such MP to be elected in this way with the support of the Catholic voters.

Continue to pick up the lovely and sylvan St Declan's Road. A highlight of the walk, this carries you over the Licky River at a pretty footbridge – which has replaced ancient stepping stones – before continuing through a hazel forest to reach the busy M25. Cross with care, and then ramble through fields and later along back roads, offering panoramic views over Ardmore. Finish spectacularly along the great sweeping beach where a large boulder known as St Declan's Stone lies. This makes a great place to connect fully with the landscape by removing your footwear and walking barefoot on the silken sands by the water's edge and perhaps dipping your feet in the salt waters.

Reshod, it is up the incline to St Declan's monastic site. Occupying a striking location, the most prominent landmarks are the 30m high round tower and the now roofless 12th century cathedral. With a lavishly ornate gable, depicting stories from the bible, this is regarded as one of Ireland's finest examples of Romanesque architecture. Next, visit the oldest building on the site which is the much smaller St Declan's Oratory within which, it is reputed the remains of St Declan lie. And this means the time has come to bask in the heart-warming satisfaction of reaching your 115km journey's end.

Note: *No pilgrim walker should consider their journey along St Declan's Way entirely complete until they have circuited the magnificent Ardmore Cliff Path. This undemanding 90-minute stroll offers spectacular coastal views and a sense of reconnecting with history. Start from outside the Cliff House Hotel which is spectacularly located on a clifftop above the ocean. Pilgrim path markers will then lead to the ruins of Declan's Hermitage, where the Saint spent the last years of his life. There is also a holy well, where the Saint is reputed to have performed many baptisms and cures.*

Beyond, the cliff-top path meanders spectacularly around Ardmore Head, with great declivities falling left to the wreck of the Sampson crane ship, which foundered in 1988. Rounding Ram Head, you will be rewarded with a photogenic vista over Youghal Bay to the east Cork coastline. Next, a stone structure built over a spring has all the appearance of an ancient holy well. Locally referred to as Father O'Donnell's Well it was, you may be somewhat disappointed to discover, built in 1928 by one T. P. O'Rahilly of Limerick, who believed strongly in the curative power of the waters issuing here. Finally, swing inland past Ardmore soccer pitch and you will soon regain St Declan's Monastery and burial place.

ARDMORE

Legend has it that a golden bell from heaven appeared while Declan was celebrating mass abroad. On the last leg of his return journey to Ireland, Declan, absent-mindedly, left it behind when he sailed from Wales and was distraught about the loss. He prayed and soon, a large floating stone carrying his bell appeared in the ocean and began guiding his boat towards Ireland. Declan promised to build a monastery wherever the bell came ashore. The rock landed on the beach of present-day Ardmore and so Declan founded Ireland's first monastery on the high ground above the beach.

History records thousands of pilgrims coming to Ardmore since at least the 17th century and particularly during the pattern day festivities taking place on St. Declan's feast day, July 24th. Beneath the Stone, there's a small hollow through which many believers would drag themselves in the hope of spiritual and bodily healing.

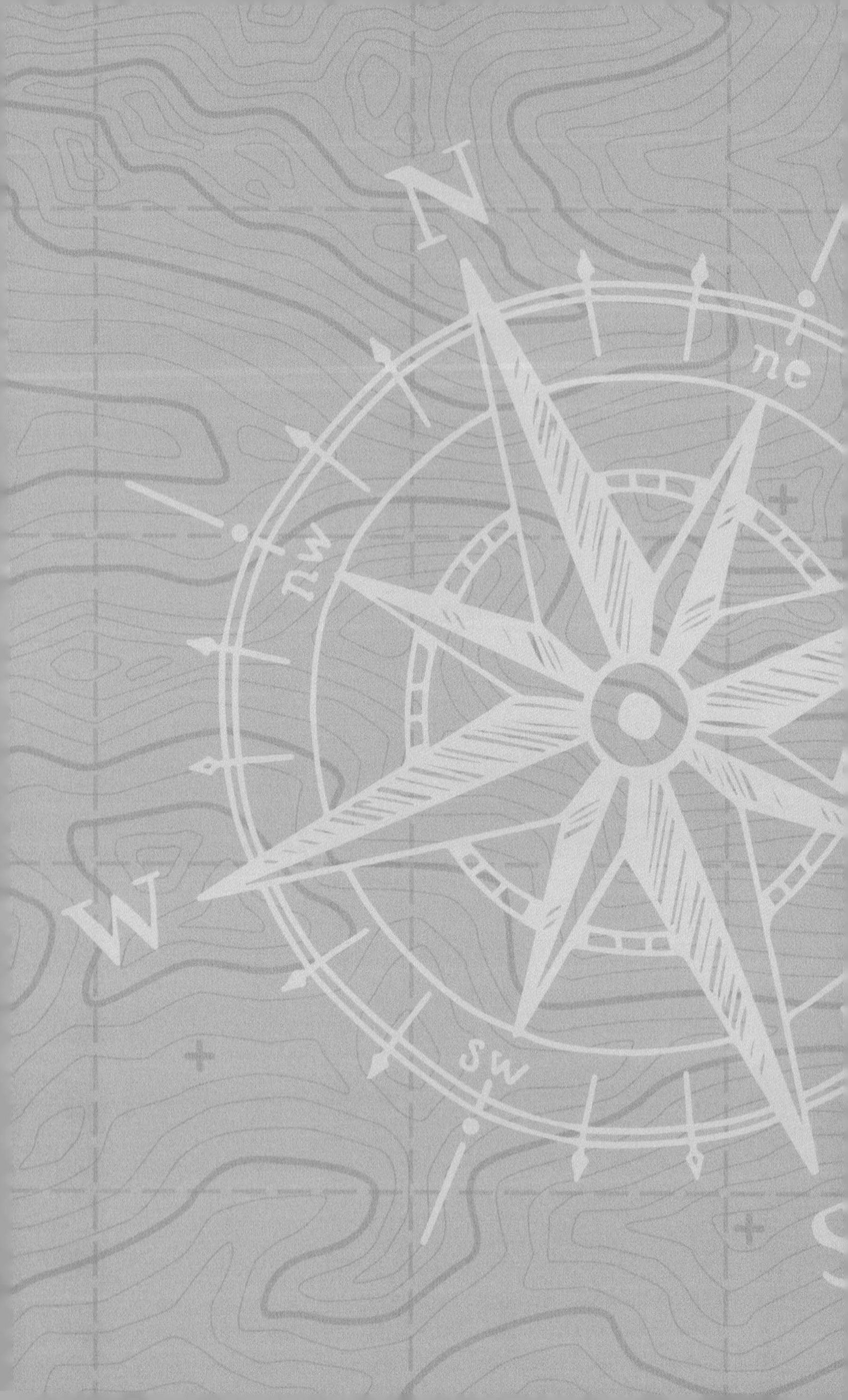
N
ne
nw
W
sw

THE PILGRIM PASSPORT JOURNEY

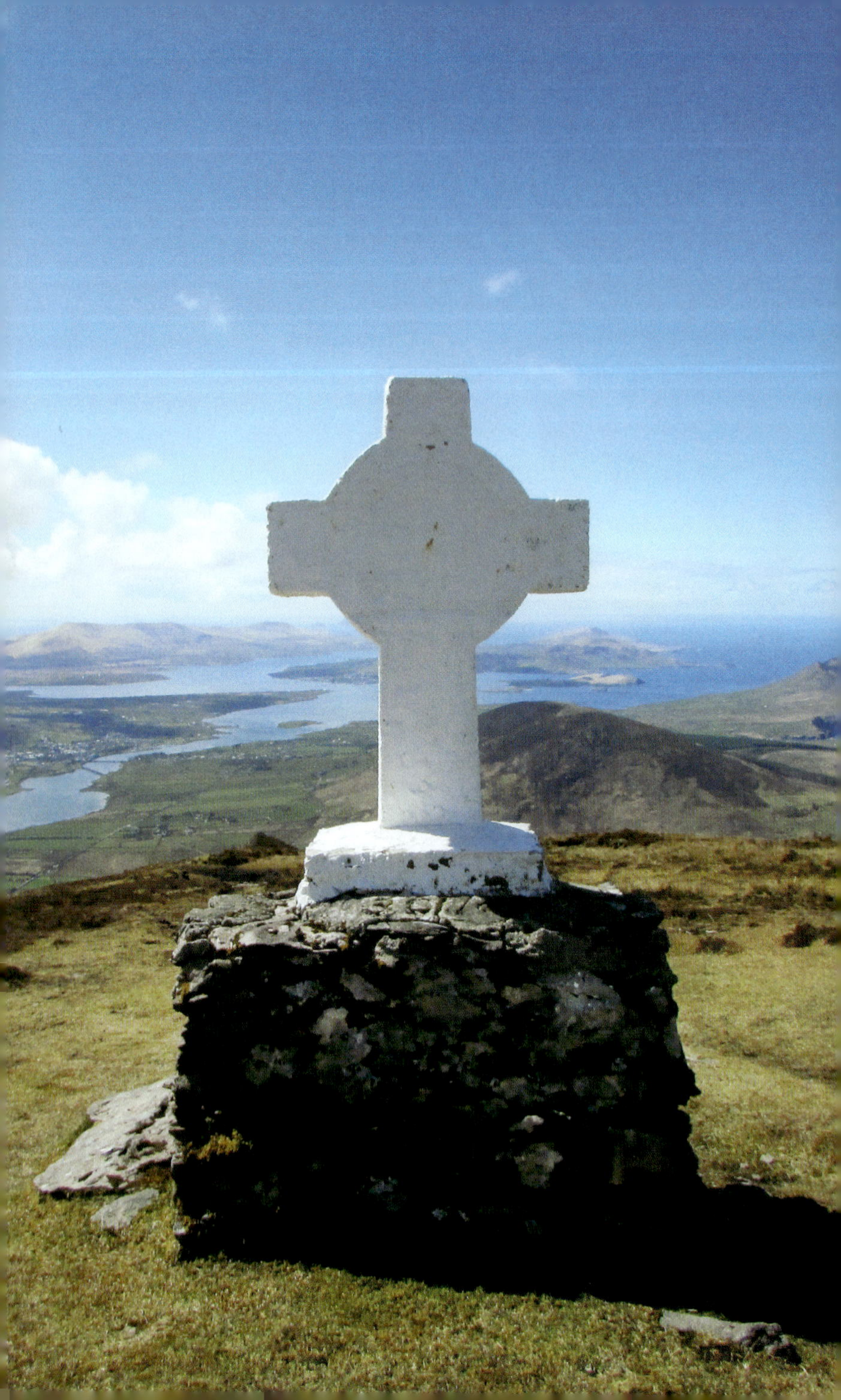

INTRODUCTION

The first recorded person to undertake an Irish Pilgrim Passport Journey was an Armagh man, Haneas MacNichaill, who, during the 16th century, was obliged to visit 19 widely dispersed places of pilgrimage in Ireland and on its offshore islands as a penance for murdering his son. Today, pilgrim walks are rarely, if ever, undertaken as a penance for sin but are done for more personal, wellness or cultural reasons.

For the modern pilgrim walker, the Irish Pilgrim Passport Journey, which is administered by Pilgrim Paths Ireland, offers an opportunity to explore five relatively short but waymarked penitential routes through captivating scenery in widely separated parts of Ireland. The ancient routes included on the Irish Pilgrim Passport are Cnoc na dTobar, Co. Kerry; Cosán na Naomh, Co. Kerry; St Finbarr's Pilgrim Path, Co. Cork; St Kevin's Way, Co. Wicklow and Tóchar Phádraig, Co. Mayo.

All routes come with a vibrant pilgrim tradition reaching to early Christian or pre-Christian Times. To fulfil the Irish Pilgrim Passport Journey requirements, participants must produce evidence of having completed 120km of Ireland's spiritual trails. This enables walkers to gain the required stamps for the Irish Pilgrim Passport in 6 or 7 days of walking and then obtain a Teastas Oilithreachta (completion certificate) from Ballintubber Abbey, Co. Mayo having completed all of the required paths. Passports may be purchased from Ballintubber Abbey, and there is no limit on the time taken to complete the full journey. Details of the locations where the passport may be stamped are to be found by visiting, pilgrimpath.ie.

03 CNOC NA dTOBAR
CO. KERRY

Overview: *A myth-laden mountain with a mystical tradition reaching back to pagan times; its summit offers expansive vistas over virtually the entire south-west of Ireland. Initially rather wet and somewhat muddy, the serpentine pilgrim path soon comes into its own. It leads from just above sea level to an enchanting summit with continually opening vistas along the ascent route. Discovery Series, map sheet 83 covers the entire route, while the nearest shops are located in nearby Cahersiveen.*

Suitability: *A there-and-back trail that is very clearly marked, starting gently and becoming more strenuous near the summit. As you are ascending to a high summit (690m) that can be windy and cold, be equipped with suitable clothing, footwear, and perhaps, walking poles, which can be particularly useful on the descent. Please note that those wishing to satisfy the requirements for obtaining the Irish Pilgrim Passport stamp need only climb to the 11th station of the cross.*

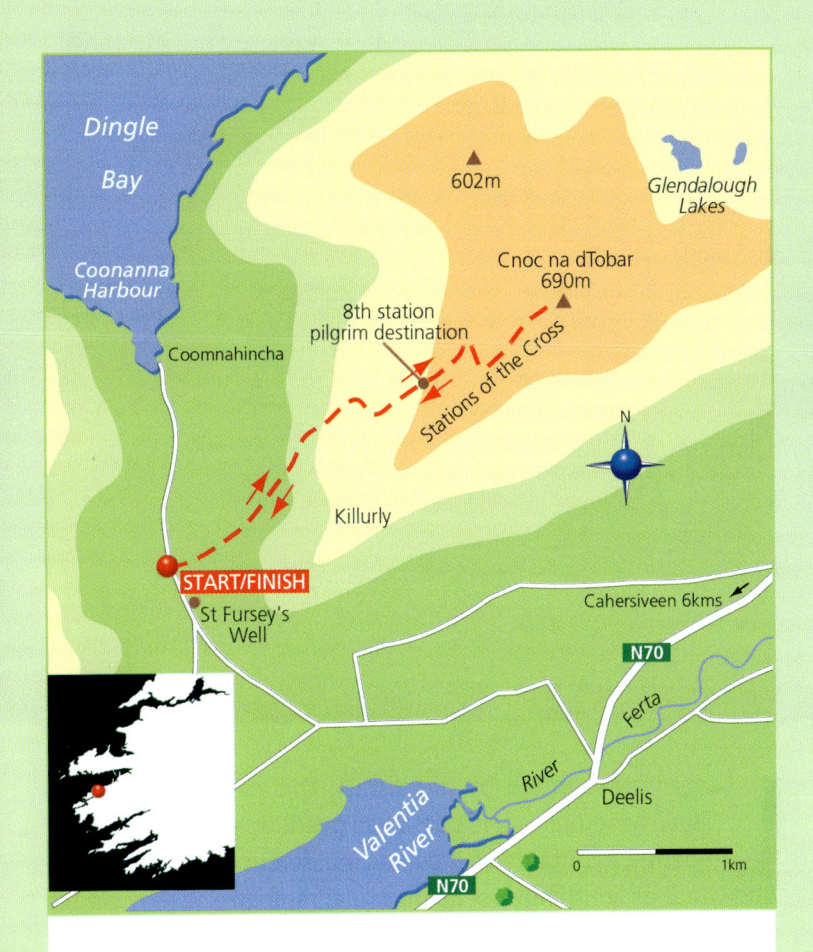

Getting there: *Turn off the N70, Ring of Kerry in Cahersiveen to cross a bridge and take the first right and second left. Pass St Fursey's Well. Park at the carpark on the right where all-day parking costs (at the time of writing), €3.00.*

Start/finish: *Cnoc na dTobar car park.*

Estimated Time: *4 hours.*

Distance: *7km (there and back).*

55

View from Cnoc na dTobar

Largely untouched by modernity, this mythical place of pagan assemblies and Lughnasa overindulgences has, until recently, maintained a dignified indifference to the hire cars and coaches scuttling past its muscular ramparts as they circuit the Ring of Kerry. Increased footfall came, however, when it was recognised, in 2014, as one of Ireland's penitential mountains.

The trail begins from the traditional start point for Cnoc na dTobar lying near St Fursey's Holy Well, which reputedly offers a cure for blindness. It then follows the convenient handrail provided by 14 stations of the cross marking the ancient summit trail. The crosses are supplemented with poles and yellow markers to ensure easy navigation. The stations were built in the 19th century by Canon Timothy Brosnan. A larger-than-life parish priest who hailed from Castleisland in North Kerry, he also

56   GREAT IRISH PILGRIM JOURNEYS

constructed the Daniel O'Connell Memorial Church in nearby Cahersiveen.

Initially, the trail is benign, if a little tedious and sometimes muddy underfoot. It crosses some wet patches and meanders a little left in an apparent effort to find the line of least resistance while expansive coastal views unfold southwest over Coonanna Harbour, Dingle Bay and twin-topped Killelan Mountain. Cnoc na dTobar has been a site of devotion to St Fursey since early Christian times when the saint was reputedly cured of blindness at the well that now bears his name.

Valentia Island is laid out below Cnoc na dTobar like a giant ship moored neatly to the Kerry coastline. It was here that football legend, Mick O'Connell was born. Overcoming the sporting handicap of living on an island, which at that time was not linked to the mainland, he won 4 All-Ireland titles with Kerry and was regarded as the greatest-ever exponent of the uniquely Irish sport of Gaelic football.

The island's other claim to fame is that it was once an unlikely epicentre of world communication. An accident of geography made this the optimum place to send the first Trans-Atlantic, electronic message, which was transmitted in 1857. The location was later considered so crucial that it was heavily fortified by British soldiers during World War 1. This did not prevent a coded message being forwarded by local nationalists in 1916, informing Irish republicans in New York that the Easter Rising had begun in Dublin.

Halfway up, the mountain reasserts itself just a little. The going steepens but never becomes really challenging as the path weaves eccentrically upwards towards the mountain's sinuous southwest ridge. It is only necessary to reach the 11th station to fulfil the requirements for obtaining a passport stamp, but in good weather, it would be a shame to miss the opportunity of going to the summit.

Soon after the 11th station, you will gain Cnoc na dTobar's sinuous south ridge. A majestic vista radiates southwest over the multiple bays and inlets around Cahersiveen and Valentia, as the ocean spectacularly drowns the Kerry landmass. Floating in the deep blue beyond is Ireland's last stand against the Atlantic – the dreamy Skellig Rocks with their world-famous monastic enclosure, which has been designated a World Heritage Site. Dursey Island tugs the eye southwards as it clings like a droplet to the fingernail of the Beara Peninsula, while further along the ridge lies a magical prospect – the unmistakeable outline of Carrauntoohil amid the angular MacGillycuddy's Reeks.

An imposing Celtic cross on the summit plateau, which is known locally as the Canon's Cross, has recently been refurbished and now acts as the modern summit destination. Clearly, the site was advisedly chosen for it offers arresting views to the other 2 sacred sites of Kerry – Mount Brandon and Skellig Michael. The extensive mountaintop was also well-chosen to host the singing, dancing, athletic contests and merrymaking associated with the ancient Festival of Lughnasa. Otherwise, it is unspectacular, for the reward hereabouts lies with distance.

The highest point lies a little further on and offers an entrancing panorama over the mountains of Dingle to the surreal outline of the Blasket Islands. Lording it over the surrounding uplands, it offers the perfect 360-degree vista, not just beautiful but hauntingly visceral. To conceive a comparable Irish mountaintop spectacle is difficult – perhaps Mount Brandon, Slieve Carr or even Errigal.

From here, you can have the option of following the ridge, above the postcard-perfect Glendalough lakes, before descending to Kells Bay on the north side of the mountain after about 4.5 hours of a linear walk. Most will take the logistically easier option of retracing their steps to the carpark, while reflecting that Cnoc na dTobar is for a clear day when the extravagant vista will remain forever stamped in the imaginings of all who aspire to its magical summit.

View from Cnoc na dTobar

DANIEL O'CONNELL

Born to a Catholic family residing in a relatively humble abode at Carhan, Co. Kerry, O'Connell grew up at a time when the profound discrimination against Catholics in Ireland was being somewhat relaxed. The ruins of his humble abode still remain just outside Cahersiveen and are visible by looking almost directly south from Cnoc na dTobar. He was lucky, however, to be raised by his wealthy, childless uncle, Maurice "Hunting Cap" O'Connell, at Derrynane House, which lies further south along the Ring of Kerry. Residing in a very secluded location, Hunting Cap made money in the only way open to those living among the infertile lands of south Kerry at this time.

Situated far from the prying eyes of the law, Derrynane proved an ideal location for smuggling goods and liquor to and from France. The wealth created here enabled Hunting Cap to provide Daniel with the best possible education. This money was well spent, for it allowed the young O'Connell to study law and then go on to become known as "The Liberator" when he won Catholic Emancipation, the right for Catholics to enter the British Parliament.

Photograph by August Schwerdtfeger / Wikimedia

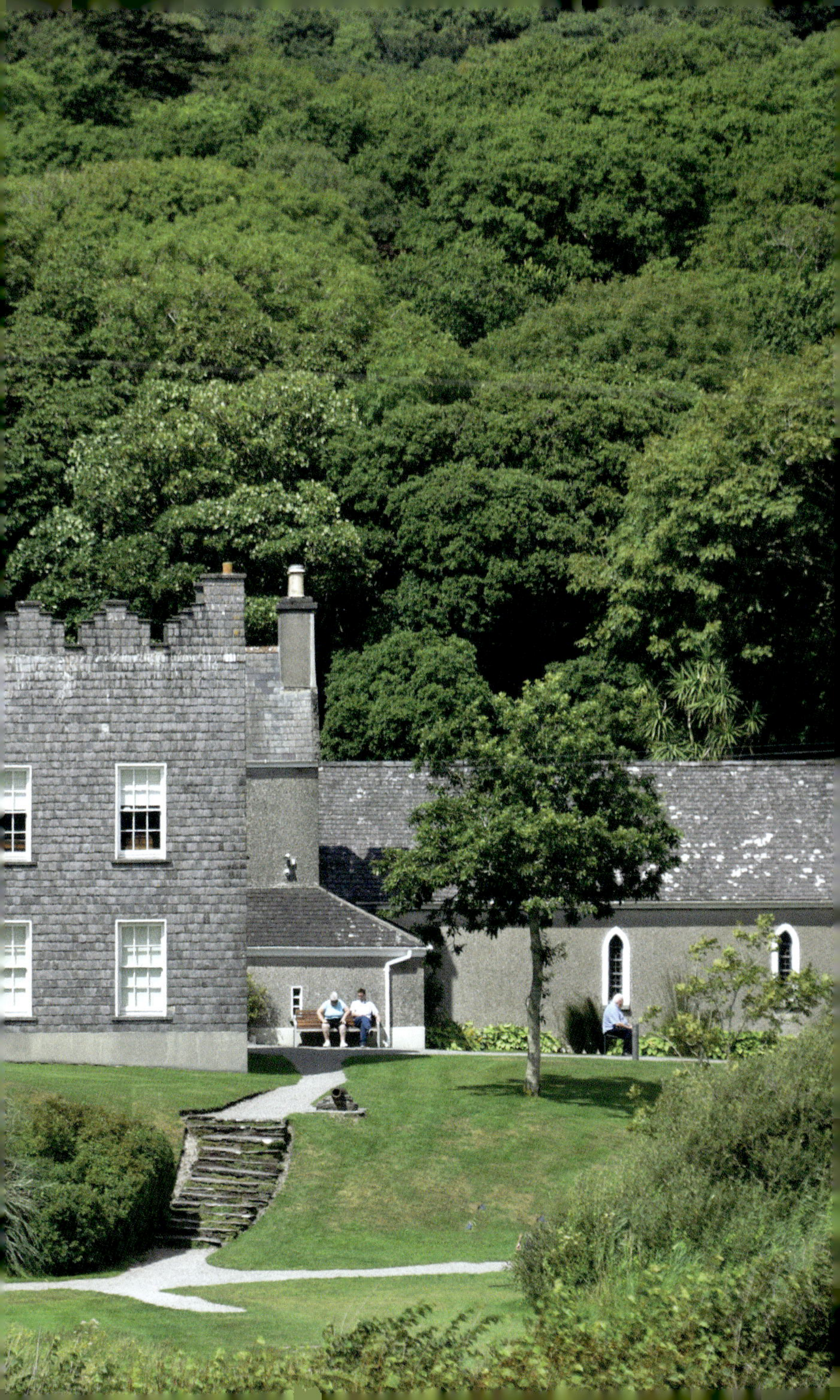

04 COSÁN na NAOMH (THE SAINTS' ROAD) CO. KERRY

Overview: *The Cosán na Naomh follows an ancient pilgrim route with a strong penitential tradition, finishing beneath one of Ireland's highest and most majestic mountains. Since the attractions here are rooted within people and place, on foot is by far the best way to experience the elemental, skeletal topography of Corca Dhuibhne in its true dimensions.*

Suitability: *A relatively unchallenging but rather lengthy linear walk requiring transport at both ends. You can purchase food at Siopa Ui Lúing in Ventry and at Gallarus Visitor Centre (Seasonal opening).*

Getting there: *Follow the R559 west from Dingle. At Ventry (Ceann Trá), swing left for the strand, where the trailhead is located.*

Start: *Ventry Beach. The Cosán na Naomh is signposted from here.*

Finish: *Ballybrack (An Baile Breac) car park.*

Estimated Time: *Allow 5 hours to complete the Cosán. Note, however; this can easily morph into a long day if time is spent exploring the many antiquities, historic buildings and religious sites along the route.*

Distance: *18km.*

63

Beneath the Atlantic skies of Corca Dhuibhne, there exists a dense concentration of ring forts, souterrains, burial chambers, clocháns and dry-stone huts. These form a vast story written in rock, available to readers of the landscape who possess the knowledge to unlock the multilayered sagas of these ancient stones. Isolated for generations by mountain and ocean, the locals unhurriedly go about the traditional businesses untroubled by tour coaches and day trippers who follow the same clockwise route around the peninsula.

According to mythology, a great battle took place here in prehistoric times with the ubiquitous Irish hero, Fionn Mac Cumhaill, reputedly defeating the emperor of the world. It is also the landscape David Lean used to make the movie Ryan's Daughter in 1970 that kick-started tourism to West Kerry. Despite a stellar cast, the real star of the film, unsurprisingly, turned out to be the beguiling Kerry landscape.

The tradition of Christian pilgrimage to Brandon Mountain dates back to the earliest times when the pagan deity Crom Dubh was reputedly ousted from his mountain fastness by St Brendan the Navigator, who some believe was the first European to reach North America. The Christian Church probably adapted the medieval pilgrimage to Brandon from an earlier pagan celebration. Certainly, the origins of the path are rooted in the fact that it was to Ventry that pilgrims arrived by boat and then walked the Saint's Road (Cosán na Naomh) to Mount Brandon and then ascended to St Brendan's Oratory on the summit. This may surprise you but it is important to remember that much medieval pilgrimage was undertaken using water transport. Ventry Beach was then the most convenient and safest landing place on an otherwise unforgiving coastline. For this reason, pilgrims journeying by sea to Mount Brandon came ashore here.

Starting from Ventry Beach, the Cosán initially dallies along a series of pleasant back roads and bucolic lanes with many

Gallarus Oratory, Dingle peninsula, Co. Kerry

echoes from the past in the form of ring forts, monastic sites and a ruined medieval castle. After a short excursion on the main Ventry to Ballyferriter road, the waymarkers lead right on a byroad that eventually transforms itself into a boreen offering dramatic views over the Three Sisters' Peninsula. A little more road walking is then followed by a serene path through small fields that, in summer, are abundant with wildflowers. Soon after, cross a road and follow a lane to reach the remarkably intact Gallarus Oratory.

Bereft of its original purpose as a community chapel, Gallarus has instead mutated into a modern place of worship for archaeology buffs and overseas tourists. Startlingly uniform and puritanically unadorned, it is about the size of a large garden shed, but entirely built of unmortared stone with an apex roof that gives it the appearance of an upturned boat. Described by the poet Seamus Heaney as "A core of old dark walled up with stone", it is in the interior twilight that it comes most to life. Its sublimely corbelled roof, which is the true glory of the place has not allowed even one drop of water enter since it was built eons ago.

COSÁN NA NAOMH

Now it's a question of making your way through the Gallarus Visitor Centre, which offers café facilities, before continuing for a short distance along a lane to the striking eminence of Gallarus Castle. Built by the Fitzgerald family in the 15th century, it has recently been restored, although technically it is not actually a castle but a tower house. These were built by wealthy landowning families both as secure refuges and as status symbols and this is one of the few surviving tower houses of this kind on the Dingle Peninsula. Like many other buildings of this kind in Ireland, it was severely damaged during the Cromwellian Wars in the 17th century.

Down a lane, then right and left on a public road will convey you to the large circular stone fort conveniently located beside the Cosán at Caherdorgan East. This early medieval cashel is well worth the tiny diversion as it contains some fine examples of the clochán style dwellings that once characterised the Dingle Peninsula. A circular enclosure, it would have been home to a fairly prosperous farming family in the early Medieval period.

Beyond, it is right again on a lane leading to the most important ecclesiastical site in the area. The centre point is Kilmalkedar's twelfth-century Hiberno-Romanesque church, which is thought to have been modelled on Cormac's Chapel at Cashel, Co. Tipperary, and is one of several stone-roofed churches that were built in Ireland during the Medieval period. The church is now roofless but this seems unimportant for the place resonates with intangible mystery and stay-awhile charm. Here, an Ogham stone beside the Romanesque church is dedicated to St Maolcéadair.

Beyond Kilmalkedar, the Reenconnell Ridge rises like a 274 m speed bump on the road to redemption. Follow the waymarkers up towards a low point on the ridge. Expansive views will open up all around as you ascend through stone-walled fields to the high point. For pilgrims past, this would have been the first close-up view over their promised land with the great rampart

▲ The Spiral Stone

of the Brandon range filling the horizon. And directly below is the defiantly untouristy Irish-speaking lands of Feohanagh – a charming backwater very close to, but removed from, the intrusions of mass tourism. At the highest point, look out for a rocky outcrop that displays a recently discovered piece of rock art. Created as a perfect spiral motif, this artifact long predates Christian pilgrimage.

On the descent, the terrain becomes noticeably rougher and more demanding, although it remains well waymarked. Eventually, the trail leads to a minor roadway beside a bungalow. Going right takes you the short distance to join the Dingle to Feohanagh main road. Going left, walk with care for a short distance along this busy highway before diverting right and soon after right again along another minor road leading the 1.5km to your journey's end at Baile Breac.

COSÁN NA NAOMH

MOUNT BRANDON

Mount Brandon, with an elevation of 924m, towers majestically above Baile Breac. It is the highest Irish mountain outside the MacGillycuddy's Reeks range and also one of the country's finest. If you would like to complete the ancient pilgrim route to Mount Brandon's summit, start by climbing upwards from Ballybrack, passing an imposing Marian Grotto that stands beside a picturesque mountain stream. Cross a bridge and continue uphill with a stream on the left to reach a gate. A little beyond this gate, veer left from the main track and follow a line of white posts uphill over another bridge to reach the first of the 14 stations of the cross that lead most of the way to the summit.

The going here is pleasant and relatively undemanding with a reassuringly well-defined path rising at a modest angle from station to station. Beyond an impressive-looking standing stone, which marks the approximate halfway point, the path veers somewhat right and the going steepens a bit but never becomes really demanding. On the approach to the summit, your path is joined by a low wall before veering left and then right again for the final push to the top, which you should reach after an ascent of 2.5 hours. Here, you will find the summit is adorned with a cross and the remains of an oratory. On a clear day, Brandon offers arresting views stretching from Carrauntoohil west to the staggeringly photogenic Blasket Islands, which were once a renowned wellspring of literary writing in the Irish language. To the north is the surreal outline of the Aran Islands, while the hills and glens of Coirce Dhuibhne are laid out directly beneath your feet. Afterward, retrace your steps along the same route to Baile Breac.

Cosán na Naomh / The Saints' Road ▶

Note: *Although the going never gets terribly tough, this is a challenging walk that reaches the summit of a high mountain. Exposure to the Atlantic means that weather changes may occur rapidly, so be well kitted out with warm clothing, food, hot drinks and raingear, along with a map and compass that you can use competently. Allow at least 4 hours for your there-and-back walk of about 7km.*

ST BRENDAN

The patron saint of Co. Kerry, he was born in Annagh, near present-day Fenit, in the 5th Century, and in an era when travel was rare, he was by far the most adventurous seafarer among the Irish Christian missionaries of the period. Ordained by St Erc, he established monasteries at Ardfert, Co. Kerry and Clonfert, Co. Galway, he reputedly Christianised the Dingle Peninsula by ousting pagan deity Crom Dubh from Mount Brandon and establishing instead a Christian oratory. He earned the soubriquet "Navigator" by sailing to Scotland, Wales and finally the northern coast of France. It is, however, for his legendary journey west from Ireland in search of the "Island Promised to the Saints", that we best know him. This was described in a popular medieval text titled Navigatio Sancti Brendan Abbatis (Voyage of Saint Brendan the Abbot), making him internationally renowned.

Tradition holds that St Brendan and his monks celebrated mass on Mount Brandon before setting out on their voyage from nearby Brandon Creek to cross the Atlantic. Immediately, this raises the question; was St Brendan the first European to reach the New World? Certainly, the Navigatio Sancti describes, with credible detail, a 7-year journey by the Saint to the "Isle of the Blessed" which could have been North America except it didn't become known as America until the much later time of Christopher Columbus.

Nobody can, of course, be certain if he succeeded in confronting the wild North Atlantic to reach the new world, but if he did, his achievement far outshines, for its sheer audacity, anything achieved by Edmund Hillary, Ernest Shackleton or Neil Armstrong and his appellation "the Navigator" was truly well-earned.

Ardfert Friary. Photograph by Laurel Lodged / Wikimedia

05 ST FINBARR'S PILGRIM PATH
CO. CORK

Overview: *In West Cork, the practice of walking a pilgrim path to St Finbarr's hermitage in Gougane Barra has been in place for many centuries. The path leads from Drimoleague, where, local tradition has it, St Finbarr arrived at the Top of the Rock in the sixth century. He admonished the people to return to Christ, before making his way to Gougane Barra, where he founded a monastery. Moving on to become a bishop, he is now indisputably accepted as the patron saint of Co. Cork, with many well-known institutions named in his honour.*

In 2008, the practice of following this ancient route was revived and, today, many groups and individuals are regularly found walking the 22-mile (35km) path. Leaving aside the spiritual aspects, this walk is also a great outing over 3 mountains and 4 valleys, namely the Ilen, Mealagh, Ouvane and Lee Valley basins. Just beyond, the route coalesces with the Beara-Breiffne Way, before leading over the Shehy Mountains to Gougane Barra.

Suitability: *Strenuous outing, taking 2 days to complete, that traverses a considerable amount of high isolated terrain. Even though the route is well marked, your walk reaches a high point of 434m on Mullaghmesha on day 1 and an altitude of 526m at Lough Fada on day 2. Here, cloud and mist can descend quickly and make navigation problematic.*

The map for the Sheep's Head Way also covers St Finbarr's Way and is available from Top of the Rock Podpark, Drimoleague.

Generally, the route is most suitable for experienced walkers equipped with good waterproof boots, gaiters, warm clothing, raingear and emergency rations and should not, in general, be attempted during the cold abbreviated days between November and March. If you are in any doubt about your abilities, you should consider joining one of the fully organized walks of the route. These are advertised at pilgrimpath.ie

Distance: *37km*

Coomanore Lough

The Great Rock

DAY 1
DRIMOLEAGUE TO KEALKILL
19KM

Overview: *From the Top of the Rock, Drimoleague, follow the signage for the Sheep's Head Way and St Finbarr's Way through Castledonovan to the Mealagh Valley and then on to the small village of Kealkill. There are spectacular views over Bantry Bay and stretches of the West Cork coastline while a rich archaeological landscape is combined with interesting folklore. Drimoleague and Kealkill both offer shopping facilities.*

Getting there: *From Cork City take the N71 to Bandon. Then take the R596 through Dunmanway to Drimoleague Village.*

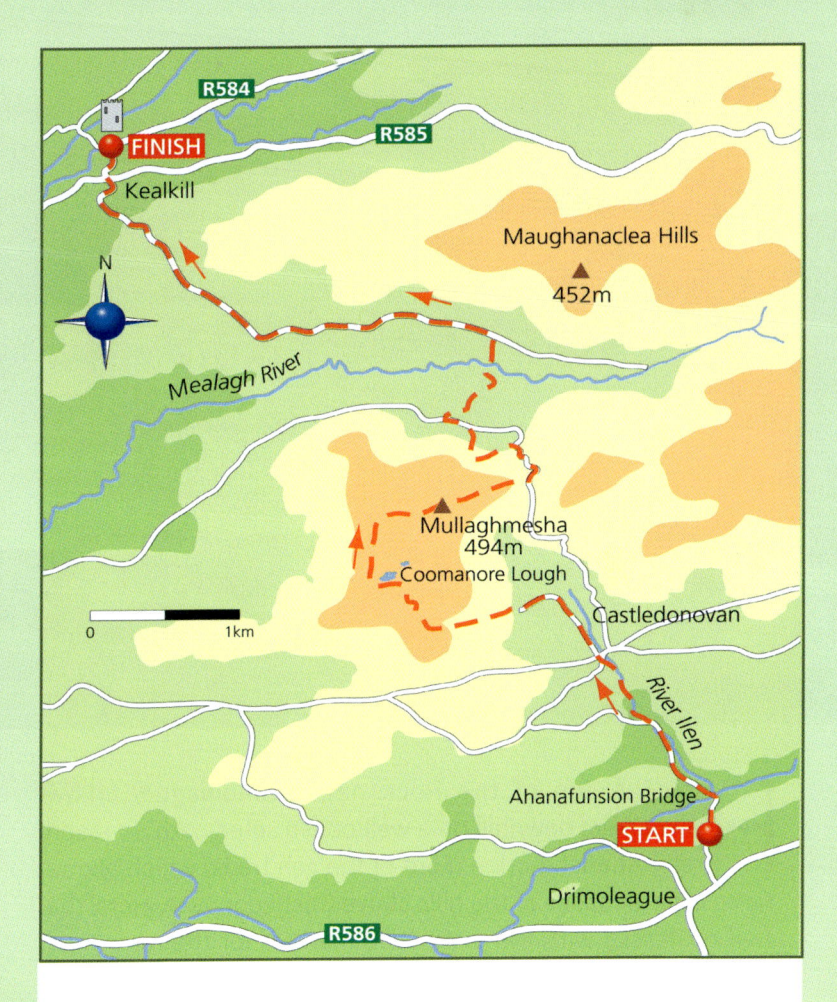

Start: *Top of the Rock, 1km north of Drimoleague.*

Finish: *Carriganass Castle, Kealkill.*

Estimated Time: *6 to 7 hours.*

Distance: *19km.*

ST FINBARR'S PILGRIM PATH

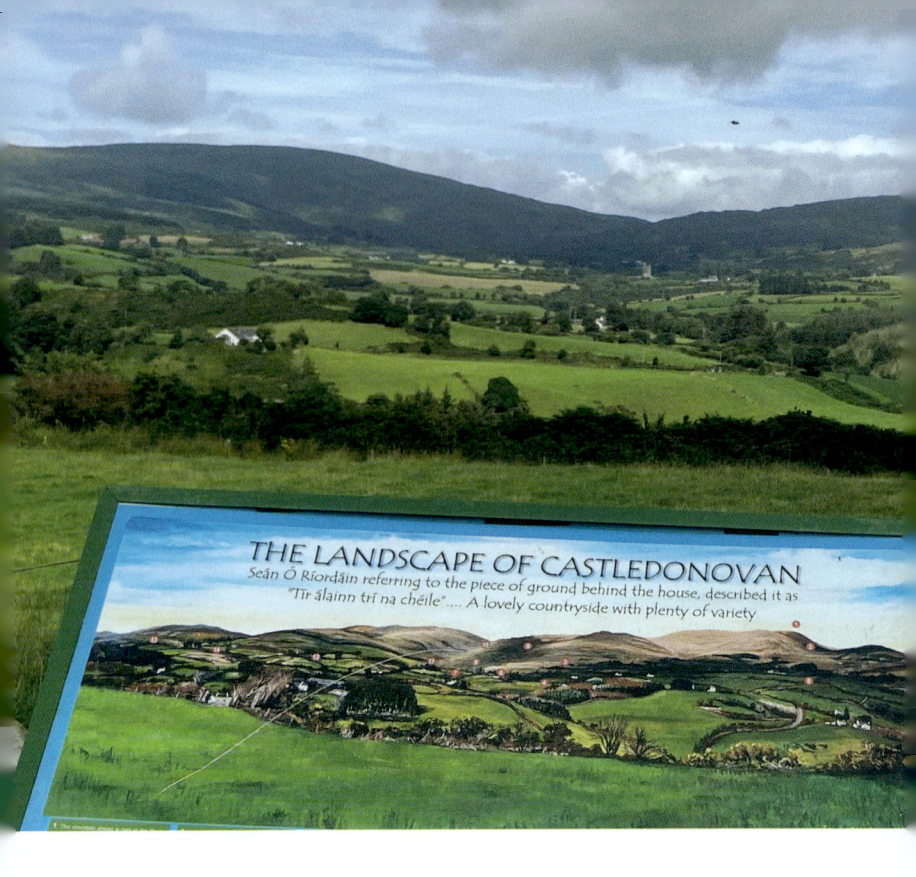

THE LANDSCAPE OF CASTLEDONOVAN
Seán Ó Ríordáin referring to the piece of ground behind the house, described it as "Tír álainn trí na chéile".... A lovely countryside with plenty of variety

From The Top of the Rock near Drimoleague, follow waymarkers downhill on a well-constructed path, to reach pretty Ahanafunction (Ford of the ash trees) which allows tantalizing glimpses of the hills above Castledonovan. Here, the trail coalesces with the distinctive markers for the renowned Sheep's Head Way East. Cross the river by stepping stones after which a short distance on a quiet road is followed by a traverse along an old mass path tagging the west bank of the River Llen.

Passing some photo-friendly cascades at Deelish, you will eventually emerge onto a tarmac road. Follow the signs to the right here for Castledonovan, which is just an intersection of roads. After about 100m go left with a great ruined castle, across the river on your right. This served as the seat of the O'Donovan clan before being damaged beyond repair by the army of Oliver Cromwell in the late 1640s. In recent years it has been consolidated and stabilized by the Irish Office of Public Works and the grounds now make a pleasant place to explore.

Continue following the footsteps of St Finbarr as you go right and uphill through remote countryside on an old bog road. Here, you will find a hidden Ireland replete with many old-style but well-maintained farmhouses painted in a pleasing vernacular white. Then, it's through a gate along a firm green road, which was constructed to facilitate turf cutting in the upland bogs.

Passing an implausibly large boulder and going on through another gate, the path then conveys you right and uphill to reveal a breathtaking lake, sitting like a reservoir amid the

ST FINBARR'S PILGRIM PATH

surrounding bogs. Now the route reaches a high point near a telecommunications mast where a sign points ahead for the house of George the Sky. George Mahony was a local hill farmer who earned this appellation by residing in a remarkably elevated house on a hillside at Glenaclothy. If you decide not to divert the short distance to see the ruins of George's airy abode, swing left and continue towards the serene Coomanore Lough. Here, you may reflect that this part of St Finbarr's Way is almost exactly as the perfect wayfarer trail should be, an evocative and timeless upland path with uplifting views and an inescapable sense of leading somewhere.

The path now leads around the western tip of the lake, where a spur route leads left for Bantry. Continue straight ahead, however, through boggy terrain to reach the western shoulder of Mullaghmesha (494m). On offer here is a panoramic view across the Meelagh Valley and southwest over the great expanse of deep water Bantry Bay shimmering to the west.

Descending in a generally northerly direction, you reach a paved road. Here, the waymarkers point across the road and on through fields to reach a minor road before continuing past the entrance to Mellagh Community Centre on the right. Soon after the way make another off-road excursion before tagging a minor road and then a lane to reach Fort Hill Road. Go left while enjoying a great panorama over Bantry Bay and the Beara Mountains beyond. Continue for about 2.5km, until a stone circle is signposted to the right. Lying only about 400m off the route, it is worth the few minutes diversion to view the Bronze Age circle accompanied by 2 much larger standing stones. From here, it is just a 2km walk through the village of Kealkill and the end of your first day's outing at Carriganass Castle, which was built as the strongpoint of the local O'Sullivan Beare chiefs in the 16th century.

THEOBALD WOLFE TONE

In 1796 a large French invasion fleet arrived to Bantry Bay with 15,000 troops on board. This was an attempt by the new French Republic to assist the Society of United Irishmen to overthrow British rule in Ireland and create an Irish Republic. On board was revolutionary Theobald Wolfe Tone, one of the leaders of the United Irishmen. An unlikely radical, he was raised an Anglican, while the majority of the United Irishmen were drawn from the oppressed Presbyterian and Catholic faiths.

Finding it impossible to land due to the weather conditions, the fleet was eventually forced to return to France with Tone ruefully commenting "England has had its luckiest escape since the Armada". Captured in 1798 while in the uniform of a French officer on board a smaller French expedition attempting to land in Donegal, he was recognised and taken to Dublin where he was tried and found guilty of treason. He died in prison on the morning he was to be executed.

View over Bantry Bay

View over Gougane Barra lake

DAY 2
KEALKILL TO GOUGANE BARRA
18KM

Overview: *A demanding route across the exposed Shehy Mountains that reaches 2 high points and an altitude of 526m at lonely Lough Fada. Services are available at Burkes shop in Kealkill, while there are nice food options at Gougane Barra.*

Getting there: *Take the N22 west from Cork city for about 28km and then go left along the R 584. Follow this through the Irish speaking villages of Inchigelagh and Ballingeary. Continue over the Keimaneigh Pass to reach Carriganass Castle after journeying about 35km from the N22.*

Start: *This section of the walk begins at Carriganass Castle, Kealkill.*

Finish: *At St Finbarr's church in the Gougane Barra Valley.*

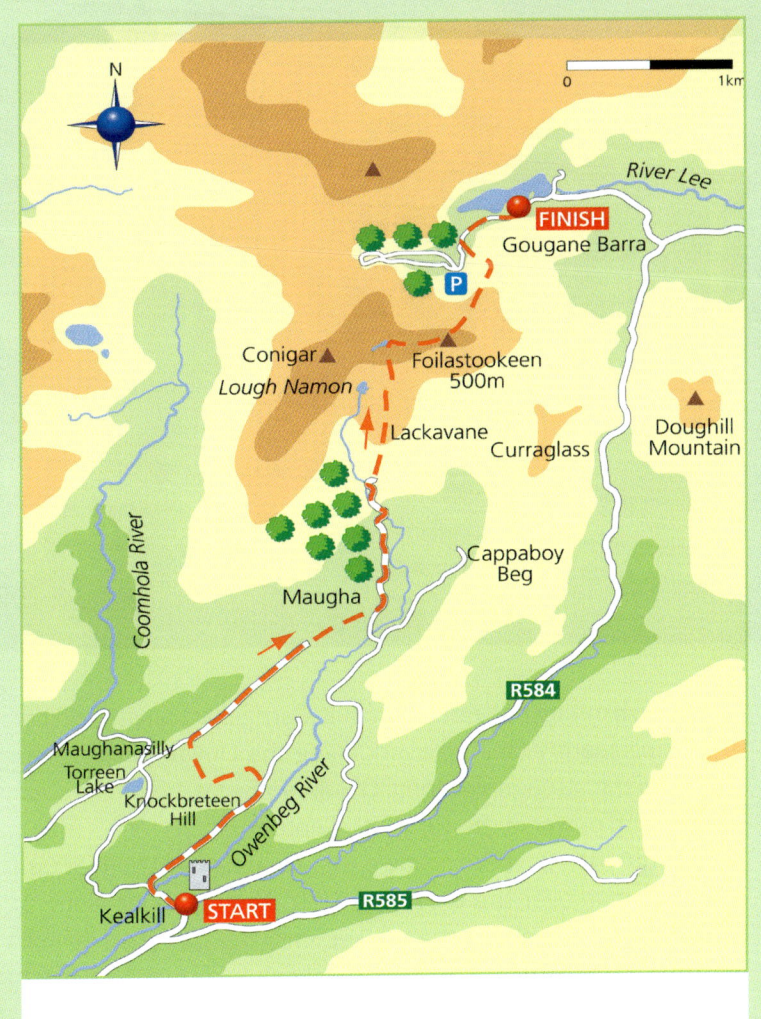

Estimate Time: *6 hours.*

Distance: *18km.*

ST FINBARR'S PILGRIM PATH 81

St Finbarr's Oratory

Today's outing begins from scenic Carriganass Castle, which is pleasantly located overlooking the Ouvane River. This was the stronghold Donal O'Sullivan Beare, before he was ousted from power in the early 17th Century.

Take the road past the castle entrance and after about 500m cross a bridge over the Owenbeg River. Then go right along a shaded byroad that gradually rises into the remotest of hill country. After about 2.5km of pleasant but unspectacular walking, leave the tarmac by a stile on the left and follow the arrows along a forest track, which then clambers sharply upwards to the summit of Knockbreteen Hill. Memorable views abound in every direction from Knockboy in the northwest (the highest mountain in Co. Cork) to the unmistakable outline of Hungry Hill adorning the southwest horizon.

Descend northwest on a steep marshy firebreak with unforgiving underfoot conditions, to a stile leading to the Maugha Road, where the route comes together with the Slí Gaeltacht Mhuscraí section of the Beara Breiffne Way and conveys you right. This follows the footsteps of Donal O'Sullivan Beare, the last great Gaelic chieftain of West Cork as he retreated north in the winter of 1603 with a thousand supporters in the hope of finding sanctuary in Ulster from the forces of Queen Elizabeth I. Follow this for about 2km. Here, waymarkers beckon you through a gateway and past a sawmill to gain open heathland on a woodland track.

Eventually, the comforting track is no more and immediately the going becomes rather soft. It's only for a short distance though and you will doubtless be glad to place your boots firmly on to the upper reaches of Lackavane Road. Now, it's just a question of swinging left with a huge wind farm filling the horizon. About 15 minutes later, having crossed a bridge over the Owenbeg River, you reach the end of the public road at an upland farm.

Follow the arrows left and past the farm buildings. Next, it's a strenuous climb across an open field and over a stile to reach a firm track leading to the Lackavane Ridge. At the end of the track, waymarkers point across open mountain to the crest of a hill. At this stage, the going is not particularly taxing and so you will be able to enjoy the splendid views over the Owenbeg River to serene Lough Namon on your left.

Cross a stile between 2 lakes and in good weather enjoy awe-inspiring views over the great Coomrua cliffs, to St. Finbarr's Church and the startlingly photogenic lake at Gougane Barra. Beyond, the route follows a fence to the right until you meet another fence going left. Follow this fence on a gentle rise to another fine viewing point on the summit of Foilastookeen (500m).

Now, tracking the invaluable markers, continue steeply down to a stile at the corner of a wood. Beyond this, you come upon a track which then doglegs down past some farm buildings. Eventually, it emerges on the floor of the valley beside an unusual-looking, but award-winning thatched toilet block.

Here it is an easy ramble up the valley to end your pilgrim odyssey with a visit to St Finbarr's Oratory, a dreamily located small church built in the late nineteenth century on an island in Gougane Barra lake. This mesmerisingly attractive lake is also the source of the River Lee, and close to where the sixth-century monastery of St Finbarr was originally located. Most walkers will then complete their day at the Gougane Barra Hotel. Its timeless allure and immutable appeal still remains, much as it was in the time when Tom Barry and his flying column dropped in from the hills above, as unexpected but welcome visitors.

THE ESCAPE OF TOM BARRY

In June 1921, the IRA's West Cork Flying Column retreated up the Borlin Valley above Bantry. The commander was the charismatic Tom Barry, who had recently rendered Cork virtually ungovernable. In pursuit were thousands of British troops while others blockaded the escape to Kerry. The position seemed hopeless until Barry embarked on his most desperate journey. He moved his men, under cover of darkness, onto the Shehy Mountains and struck out for Gougane Barra, which lay beyond the British blockade on the Keimaneigh Pass.

Eventually, he reached Poll – a steep defile that narrows to an unstable gully. Somehow, the volunteers slithered down, supported by their rifles and some ropes. An hour later "bruised and wrenched" they reached the valley and soon after were enjoying the hospitality of Cronin's Hotel as British forces abandoned the blockade having been outwitted once again.

Tom Barry / Wikimedia

06 ST KEVIN'S WAY
CO. WICKLOW

DAY 1
HOLLYWOOD TO GLENDALOUGH
27KM

Overview: *The pilgrim trail from Hollywood to Glendalough follows well-marked tracks that rise gently to a height of 460m at the Wicklow Gap and then descends benignly to the finish at the ancient monastic ruins. Hollywood is served by a nice café, while there is a shop nearby the village. Food is available at Glendalough. Those who abominate road walking might be best served by starting their journey from Ballinagee Bridge, which is located on the R756. From this point, the amount of road walking is reduced to almost zero and all the most scenic vistas still lie ahead. As this is a linear route, you will need a car pre-placed at the finish in Glendalough. Otherwise, a friend or a taxi is* required to collect and drop you back to the start point in Hollywood. Discovery map sheet 56 covers the entire route.

Suitability: *Generally, presents no objective dangers or navigational difficulties, except the problem of sharing a footpath-less road for about 1.5km with fast moving cars. As always, walkers should have boots, warm clothing and, of course, rainwear.*

Getting there: *Take the N81 from Dublin or the R411 from Naas through Ballymore Eustace to the small Wicklow village of Hollywood.*

Start: *The trailhead for St Kevin's Way is at the centre of Hollywood village.*

Finish: *The ancient Christian monastery at Glendalough.*

Estimated Time: *7.5 hours.*

Distance: *27km.*

St Kevin's Chair

From the quiet charm of Hollywood village, St Kevin's Way follows a picturesque glen, passing an abandoned quarry, a statue that is reputedly of the Saint and the cave where he is supposed to have slept as he made his way to Glendalough. There is also a chair shaped rock where Kevin is reputed to have taken a break from his saintly quest. Next comes a short walk on a public road after which you turn left onto a laneway and a long uphill climb for about 1.5km. Here, the route morphs into a somewhat wider road at a point offering splendid views south over Hollywood Glen to Church Mountain. The huge summit cairn atop this eminence contains the remains of the eponymous church that was an important pilgrimage site up to the eighteenth century. A more benign road now leads directly back to the busy R756, about 2km outside Hollywood.

This may surprise you but it is a general truism that early pilgrims usually followed the line of least resistance in their penitential journeys for they sought, after all, not fitness, flat tummies or sublime scenery but the quickest and easiest way to spiritual renewal at the destination. These rights-of-way, used by travellers in the early medieval period eventually morphed into modern high-speed, tarmac roads to accommodate the seemingly insatiable demands of the motor car. So, it is probable that pilgrims would have come along the direct route through the Wicklow Gap in times past.

After a couple of kilometres, you will doubtless be glad to find the trail diving onto a sinuous minor road leading right. At the end of the road, the trail passes through a farmyard and continues through a field before entering a forest. Beyond the trees, the route veers left to reach the bank of the King's River, which offers pleasant going along the riverside. Next, the waymarkers lead across a concrete bridge over the King's River and along a forest road to rejoin the R756. Here, St Kevin's Way doubles back a little confusingly towards Hollywood, by paralleling the road before reaching Ballinagee Bridge and joining with the pilgrim path coming from Valleymount.

Now the fun begins: the trail plays hide-and-seek with the main road as it ascends to the walk's highest elevation at the Wicklow Gap by diving abruptly in and out of what are mostly stands of conifers. First, it enters woodlands on the north side of the road and follows a forest roadway for about 100m until the way markers lead right and uphill along an enclosed greenway. Then the forest suddenly parts to reveal the ancient field system surrounding an abandoned farmstead. Crossing the fields behind the abandoned farmhouse makes for a pleasant diversion from forestry.

Tag a forest firebreak and continue through some mixed woodland to regain the R756 after about a kilometre. Immediately afterwards, your route departs the highway but on the south side this time. Here the going is agreeable, if unspectacular, as the path periodically enters and emerges from dense forestry. A couple of pretty wooden footbridges and a narrow boardwalk has been added here to assist your crossing of streams and boggier sections. A nice place to take a break here is at St Kevin's Pool where the Saint is reputed to have rested on his journey to Clonmacnoise.

Formed by the broadening of the King's River into a tiny little lake, it makes a great place to refresh by dipping your feet in the clear, cold waters as St Kevin is reputed to have done. Soon after, the route parallels the R756 before reaching the high point of the Wicklow Gap. Here, you can savour a vista across sweeping mountain and moorland, to rival the best the West of Ireland has to offer.

From the Gap, a pleasant if rather soggy trail conveys you downhill before crossing the road to Lough Nahanagan and then skirting a forest. Here, ancient flagstones of the old pilgrim path are still visible as a physical link to the early Christian past. Beyond these, the route crosses a stile to join a gravel track leading across a stream to the main R756.

Then it is off-road again at a scenic bridge for a spectacular descent into Glendasan. Soon after you will reach the extensive ruins of a lead mine that thrived at the middle of the 19th century. This gave valuable local employment at the time and demonstrates clearly that the potato famine did not strike evenly across all areas of Ireland. During the worst of the crisis, these mines kept starvation at bay by employing up to 200 men.

St Kevin's Pool

Next, the path follows the right bank of the Glendasan River. Passing a couple of Christian retreat houses, by the riverside on a compelling sylvan track leading to the haunting and once very secluded valley where Saint Kevin spent his life in prayer and contemplation, which later grew into an extensive monastic city. Here is a truly intimate grandeur where the landscape possesses near-perfect harmony as if created by an all-powerful heavenly architect.

ST KEVIN

According to tradition, St Kevin first lived in a monastery at Kilnamanagh, which lies outside present-day Dublin. Later he moved to the wild fastness of Glendalough in search of seclusion for uninterrupted prayer and mortification of the flesh. His companions were the animals and birds around him. Paradoxically, his wish for solitude and his reputation for holiness attracted large numbers of followers to his place of escape and a monastery was thus founded.

After Kevin died in 618, Glendalough developed into an impressive monastic city, which continued as a centre of piety and learning that rivalled Clonmacnoise. The torch of learning burned brightly here for many centuries, with medieval travellers coming to Ireland from abroad, not only to visit Kevin's tomb but also to imbibe of cutting-edge scholarship at the monastery. Further encouragement came their way when the pope promulgated a kind of medieval '7 for 1 special offer' with regard to indulgences, which offered a partial remission of punishment for sins committed. He declared that seven visits to Glendalough would equal one to Rome in terms of the number of indulgences gained, which must have been very convenient for any indulgence seekers living in Co. Wicklow.

Kevin of Glendalough was canonized by Pope Pius X in 1903 as an official saint of the Catholic Church.

St Kevin's Church, Glendalough. Photograph © Paula O'Nolan

DAY 2
VALLEYMOUNT TO GLENDALOUGH
20KM

Overview: In medieval times not all pilgrims would have travelled from the same direction to their destination. In the case of St Kevins Way, tradition holds that some would have come via Valleymount, which would make sense for anyone coming from northern parts of Ireland. This route is now waymarked and offers a shorter and more pleasant alternative to the route from Hollywood as it avoids the busy section of the R756 mentioned previously. After you have walked about 6km, the route coalesces at Ballinagee Bridge with the path coming from Hollywood.

Suitability: Surprisingly little is lost by the fact that the Valleymount Pilgrim Spur almost entirely follows public roads. The linear nature of the route and the fact that these roads are little frequented and highly scenic makes for a surprisingly contemplative and rewarding outing. Some forest tracks are then walked on your final approach to Ballinagee Bridge.

Getting there: From Blessington, Co. Wicklow, take the N81 towards Hollywood. Take the R758 left. Continue over a bridge offering great views of Blessington Lake to reach Valleymount.

Start: St Joseph's Church, Valleymount.

Finish: Glendalough Monastic site.

Estimated Time: 6 hours to Glendalough.

Distance: 20km to Glendalough.

Your walk begins from outside St Joseph's Church, which was built during the Catholic resurgence of the 19th century in Ireland and is incongruously adorned with a Latin American façade. Head south and once outside the village, you will come upon an old sweat house on the left that whispers of forgotten history. Reaching back to Celtic times, the forerunner of the modern sauna was heated to a high temperature by an open fire. For those who could endure the intense heat, it was considered a cure for joint pain and would doubtless have been ideal for weary travellers on demanding journeys.

Uphill now on a minor road with steep declivities tumbling over green pastures to the great liquid expanse of Blessington Lake. This isn't a natural body of water, however, but was created in the 1930s for both water supply and electricity generation. This was achieved by damming the Poulaphouca Waterfall on the River Liffey and drowning 5,600 acres around Valleymount, which would almost certainly have created a huge uproar today. But those were different times. Seemingly without any great fuss, over seventy families were displaced from the valley and rehoused elsewhere to create this huge reservoir supplying Dublin with drinking water.

Near the highest point, watch out for a cross inscribed stone on the right, these were a common feature of many medieval pilgrim routes. The way now descends in a Valley mount sweeping parabola, reminiscent of some remote parts of the Spanish Camino. Here, expansive prospects open up over the serene Wicklow Hills with the head of Lugnaquilla, (Leinster's highest mountain) peeping beyond.

Go left when the trail follows a firebreak. Then join a firmer trail through mixed forestry leading to Ballinagee Bridge, on the main Hollywood to Laragh Road where you join with the path coming from Hollywood and follow the route to Glendalough as described in the previous chapter.

07 TÓCHAR PHÁDRAIG
CO. MAYO

Overview: *Originally a prehistoric druidical pathway, the Tóchar still holds many resonances from the pagan past. With a history reaching back to the Bronze Age celebration of the Lughnasa Festival on its summit, it is arguably one of the oldest pilgrim paths in Europe. Reputed to have been Christianised by St Patrick, it remains stubbornly untamed and much as it was for medieval pilgrims. The route can be completed in one very challenging, or two more leisurely days, by breaking the journey at Aughagower. It is important to note that the Tóchar Phádraig does not lead to Croagh Patrick's summit, but instead crosses the east shoulder of the mountain before descending to the large car park at Murrisk.*

A map of the entire path is available from Ballintubber Abbey. Discovery map sheets 30 and 38 also cover the route. Be warned, however, that at the time of writing the Discovery Series maps do not show the correct route of the Tóchar Phádraig as it approaches Croagh Patrick.

Suitability: *Low-level walk that is generally well way-marked but there are some tough, unsanatised underfoot conditions in places. The route rises to an altitude of almost 500m on Croagh Patrick, which may prove demanding after a long day.*

Start: *Ballintubber Abbey is located just off the N84 about 14km from Castlebar. Here you must register for the Tóchar walk. This costs €15 per person. Walking alone is not allowed and you must be accompanied by at least one other person.*

Finish: *Car park at Murrisk, which is situated 8kms to the west of Westport, on the coast road to Louisburgh.*

Estimated Time: *10 hours (entire route).*

Distance: *30km.*

The Tóchar Phádraig was part of the royal road leading from Rath Cruachan, the seat of the Kings of Connaught to Cruachan Aigle the ancient name for Croagh Patrick, which even in pagan times was venerated as a sacred mountain. Later, St Patrick came this way to fast on Croagh Patrick's summit for forty days and apparently whiled away some of this time by driving all the snakes out of Ireland, which is probably a metaphor that was later created to represent banishing evil. Almost immediately, pilgrims began to follow that same road to the holy mountain. Over time the route became known as the Tóchar Phádraig or St Patrick's Causeway. Ballintubber Abbey was built on the route in 1216 on the shores of Lough Carra under the patronage of Cathal O'Conor, King of Connacht. As such, it is

Tóchar Phádraig pilgrim path

the only church still in use, which was founded by an Irish King. The Abbey soon became a prosperous place and held 3,000 acres of the best east Mayo land.

In the medieval period, it became an important overnight stop for pilgrims making their way along the Tóchar to Croagh Patrick. A hostel was put in place for pilgrims at the abbey who then traditionally embarked from here on the final section of their journey. Originally an Augustinian Friary, the Abbey suffered confiscation of its lands by King James 1 in the 17th century. This was followed by the burning of most of the buildings by Cromwellian soldiers in the mid-17th century. But the church escaped destruction and has continued unbroken as a place of worship ever since. Restoration work in the 20th century

TÓCHAR PHÁDRAIG   99

rebirthed much of the abbey to near its former glory. Since then, it has become a popular venue for celebrity marriages including that of James Bond star Pierce Brosnan.

In the 16th century, the Tóchar fell into disuse and was finally abandoned when penal laws were enacted against the Catholic religion in the early 18th century, but the route never passed from local memory. And it was here that the first stirring in Ireland's modern pilgrim era took place with the appointment of Fr Frank Fahey to Ballintubber Abbey in 1986. With the enthusiasm and energy for which he is legendary, Fr Frank immediately set about restoring the ancient Tóchar Phádraig from Ballintubber Abbey to Croagh Patrick. Landowners along the trail gave consent and the route was re-opened in 1988 and has enjoyed ever-increasing footfall in the intervening years.

Leaving the abbey grounds, you pass the remains of the baths where weary pilgrims once rested and bathed their feet on their return from a barefoot round trip to Croagh Patrick. The baths were known as the Dancora, which means 'the Bath of the Righteous' and were reputedly where the faithful ritually expressed a cleansing from all sin before returning to their homes with a changed heart. This acts as a reminder, that medieval spiritual expeditions were – unlike today when it is universally considered acceptable for returning pilgrims to use mechanised transport – very much 2-way affairs. When pilgrims reached their destination and collected their indulgences, they then had to find the motivation to face the rigours of the fatiguing plod home, all done without assistance from such self-indulgent modern-day fripperies as boots, Thousand-Mile socks, Gore-Tex jackets and high energy drinks.

In the first field, cobbled stones are still clearly exposed that were originally part of the ancient Tóchar. Then, it is on through small fields with abundant wildflowers in summer that remain much as they would have been in ancient times when, lured by the promise of immortality, medieval pilgrims trod this selfsame trail.

A left turn now takes you over several stiles and across a footbridge to gain the N84 Galway/Castlebar Road. Crossing the road with care, it is on through Castlepark Wood, a pleasant hazel forest, to reach the Ballintubber/Killavala Road near the entrance to Lufferton House. This edifice, which replaced an earlier thirteenth-century castle, is reputed to have been built with stone imported from Scotland.

After a short road walk, the route dives suddenly into the wildest of wild Mayo countryside. Rural and raw, it is now a series of rough fields alternating with forest as the wandering path crosses many minor roads and streams before eventually rejoining the Ballintubber/Killavala Road. Following the signs pointing left, you now tag the road for about a kilometre, passing the abandoned mill at Killawullaun. This was originally built to grind flax and corn. Just beyond, the arrows point right and cross country to the wildflower-rich banks of the Aille River, which remain much as they were when pilgrims passed this way.

When the waymarkers abandon the Aille, the route climbs to higher ground and you are rewarded here with a 'wow' moment: standing straight ahead is Ireland's holiest and arguably most handsome hill. Surely a moment of joyful epiphany for fatigued medieval pilgrims and today an excellent place to pause awhile and in summertime just smell the flowers. From this vantage point, Croagh Patrick reveals itself as the perfect quartzite cone, dominating the landscape with the striking shape and reputation for spirituality that attracts up to 10,000 penitents on Reek Sunday, which falls on the last Sunday of July each year.

Now the trail meanders past the poignant remains of a Famine graveyard at Bellaburke, where victims of this great tragedy were hastily buried, mostly without coffins. This is a reminder that here is area still haunted by the poignant ghosts of this sad period in

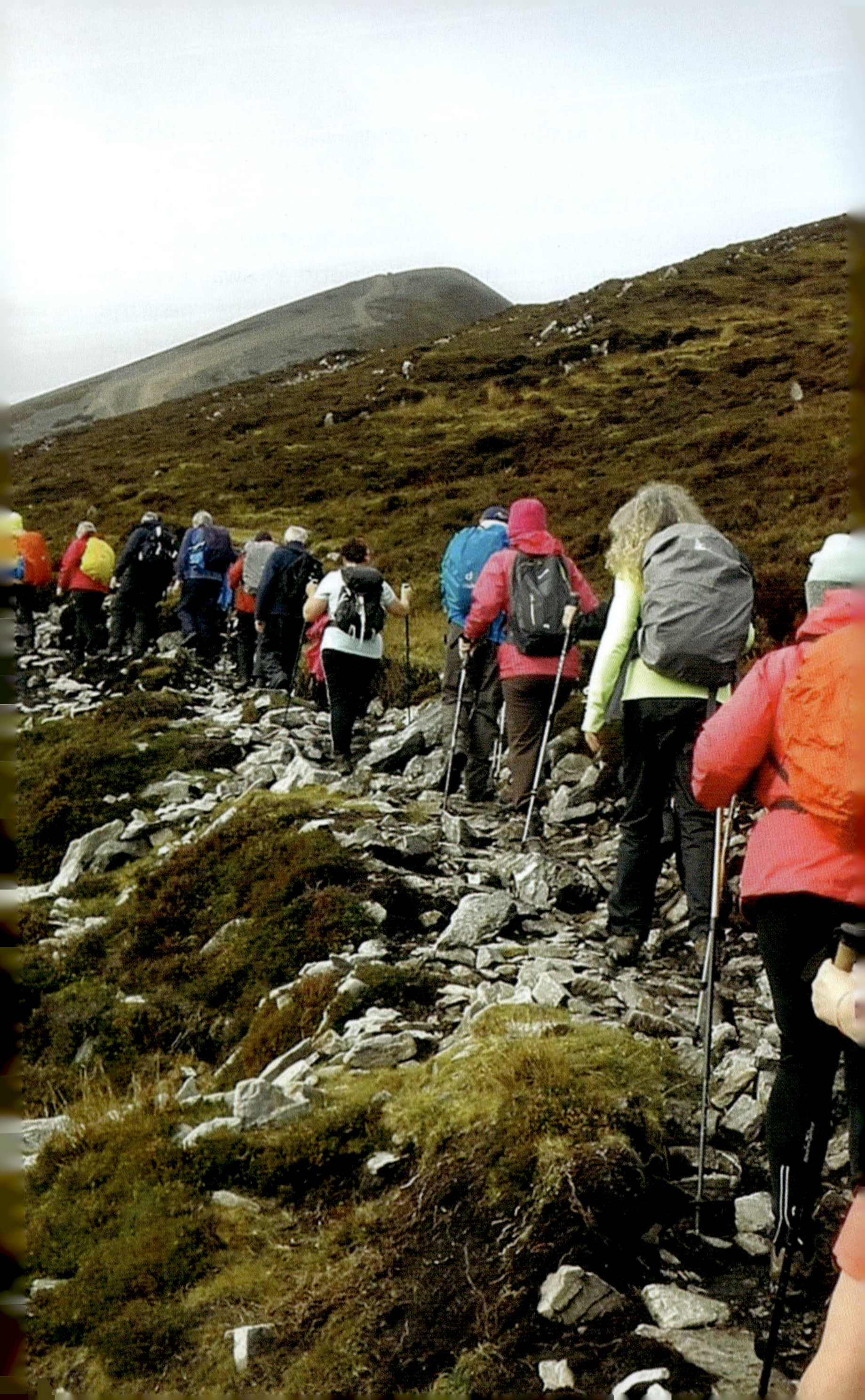

Irish history; an already impoverished locality, it lost two-thirds of its population in the decade between 1841 and 1851 and was the worst hit in all of Ireland.

Onwards now through a storybook landscape filled with ancient ritualistic sites that are sometimes swallowed by luxuriant vegetation. Here, it seems every wood, lane, massrock and holy well comes laden with a compelling saga. The jewels of Connacht are, for example, reputed to be secreted nearby the route in caves beneath the cliffs of Aille. This certainly has a ring of truth since the surface is unstable hereabouts with several examples of the land collapsing into subterranean river caves. Information on the many antiquities to be found along the route are contained in a guidebook titled, "Tóchar Phádraig – A Pilgrim Progress" which is available from Ballintubber Abbey.

Crossing another road, the path traverses the viewing point of Cloondachon Hill before descending into picturesque Aughagower, which contains an early medieval church and the remains of a 10th-century round tower. What will probably seem more important right now is the fact that it also contains a shop and a post-office with a comfortable pub to the rear.

Leave Aughagower along a minor road running past a cemetery with spectacular views of Croagh Patrick on your right. For about 7km, you now share the route with the Croagh Patrick Heritage Trail coming from Balla. Soon the path swings left and follows a leafy lane to reach a minor road. Here, the direction is to the right along a tarred road with the terrain now changing noticeably; for about 5km you will be footing serene, hedge-lined back roads.

Eventually the route swings right along tiny lanes to reach the Boheh Stone, where you part company with the Croagh Patrick Heritage Trail. Incongruously sited behind a derelict house. this natural outcrop displays one of the finest examples of Neolithic rock art within Ireland. This was once a scene of druidic worship but was later reputed to have been a massrock used by St Patrick when he Christianised the route. On April 18 and August 24, the sun, when viewed from the Boheh Stone, begins setting on the summit of Croagh Patrick and then appears to roll down the north side of the mountain in a phenomenon known as the rolling sun.

One last excursion through small fields and a crossing of the Owenwee River brings you to a tiny road skirting the striking emptiness of Croagh Patrick's south face soaring above. This leads to a base for Mayo Mountain Rescue. Here the route clambers offroad and steeply uphill on a trail that may prove tiring and demanding after a long day. It is a relatively short ascent, however, and soon you gain the path on the east shoulder of the mountain that, at almost any time, is likely to be busy with walkers either ascending towards or descending from the summit. Here, the pilgrim route swings right and descends along a stony and eroded track to journeys end at Murrisk.

Note: *In the past Croagh Patrick was a genuinely penitential and often dangerous experience for climbers because of shockingly bad under foot conditions on the approach to the summit. The famous ball-bearing screes that led to many injuries, particularly on the descent, are thankfully no more. A new 2m-wide path was built by hand over three years using vernacular materials from the mountain itself. If you decide to climb onto the mountaintop, you can now use the new steps built at all the steepest places to facilitate assent and descent.*

It is, nevertheless a bit of a puff involving a height gain of about 250m to reach the summit. Before attempting it, you will need to feel strong after a long day. It is probably a better option for those who have walked the Tóchar over 2 days and started their second day from Aughagower. You should also be aware that climbing to the summit will lengthen your day by about 90 minutes to 2 hours, so be aware of the time the light will begin fading.

SEÁN NA SAGART

In Ireland's penal times, Catholic priests and bishops had, in common with wolves, a price on their heads. This sometimes proved an irresistible temptation for poor people who perceived easy money if they became priest hunters. One such was known as Seán na Sagart. It is said that Seán, whose name was John Malowney, was responsible for the capture of several priests in Mayo and then claiming the price on their heads. Stabbed to death by a local man while trying to detain a priest, his body was thrown into a lake by local people. The priest, Seán had tried to detain, ordered, however, that the body be taken from the lake and given a Christian burial. Seán was then buried in Ballintubber Abbey grounds, but in a mark of disrespect, he was faced north so that he would never see the rising sun. A local tradition holds that an ash tree grew up soon and split his grave. This part of the story certainly holds, since a large ash tree has grown up from the grave and split the great concrete slab above the tomb. Make sure to see his grave before setting out on your journey.

Andreas F. Borchert / Wikimedia

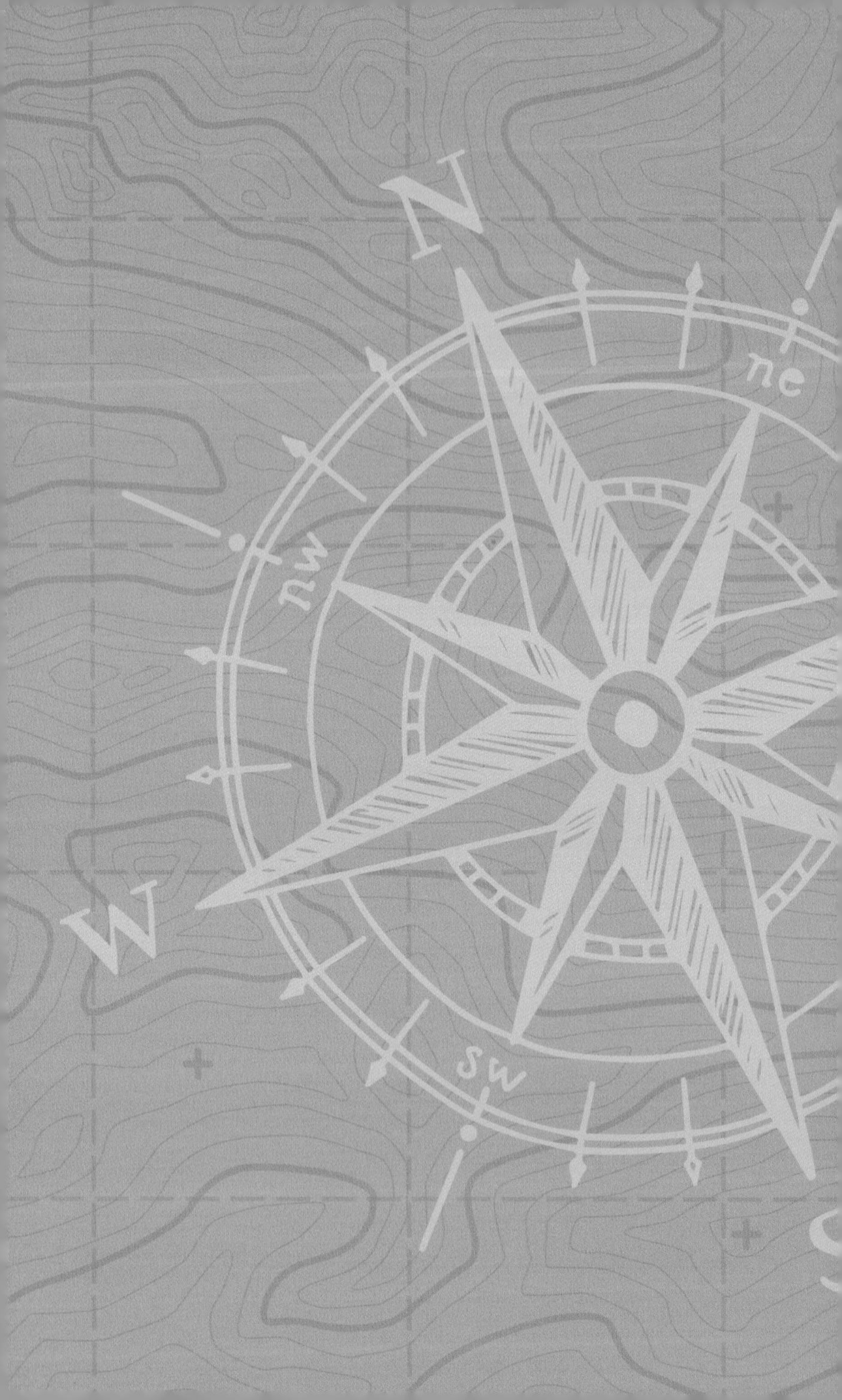
N
ne
nw
W
sw

THE CELTIC CAMINO

INTRODUCTION

Like most endeavours, pilgrimage involves restless human beings pushing back the frontiers of the possible. The coming of Christianity to Ireland during the 5th century significantly pushed back the frontiers for Irish people. Immediately creating a more stable society, it also made individuals aware of places beyond their immediate surroundings. Soon people were venturing further afield and going on pilgrimage to places associated with new Christian saints: Glendalough, Clonmacnoise, Croagh Patrick, Kildare, Gougane Barra, and Ardmore.

As travel became better organised and safer due to advances in navigation techniques during the later Medieval Age, a yearning developed among Irish people to go on pilgrimage to the 3 great pilgrim destinations of the medieval period: Rome, Jerusalem and Santiago. Of these, the Spanish city was the most easily accessible for Irish penitents and also the safest and least expensive journey. It is, however, a common belief that in making their way to the tomb of St James, penitents from Ireland walked through England and France with only short sea journeys involved. In general, this was not the case; the fastest way to Santiago was direct to Spain by sea, and only the poorest people were obliged to walk. Footing it could be dangerous, as the 100 Years War raged in France during the 14th and 15th centuries. Those of some means mostly found passage on merchant ships plying the busy trade route to the Spanish coastal city of A Coruña, having travelled from their home to Irish ports such as Dublin, Dingle, Kinsale, Waterford, Drogheda and Wexford. On arrival in Spain, they walked or perhaps hired horse transport for the relatively short distance to Santiago.

With the great re-awakening of pilgrim walking in Spain during the late 20th century, the Cathedral of Santiago decreed in 1990 that to obtain a Compostela (completion certificate for a self-propelled journey to Santiago), a pilgrim had to walk at least 100km on any route leading to the shrine of St James. This worked fine for most routes, but the A Coruña to Santiago path was just 75km. No Compostela could, therefore, be issued with the result that the route declined in popularity.

During 2016, the policy was changed. In a move that has diverted Camino spending to the Irish countryside, the Cathedral of Santiago agreed it would now count a pilgrim path walked in Ireland before arriving in Spain. The certificate issued for completing 25km on an Irish pilgrim path could now be taken to A Coruña and combined with a further 75km walk in Spain to receive the full Camino Compostela from the Santiago Pilgrim Office. In this regard, the Irish Camino Society has been designated to provide certification that the required walk has been undertaken.

Titled the Celtic Camino, and sometimes known as the "Seafarers Route", the newly revitalised path has proven particularly attractive to those with busy working lives; the Spanish section is a comfortable 4-day walk, while the required pilgrimage in Ireland involves just a one-day outing.

OVERVIEW

If you wish to complete the Celtic Camino, start with a pilgrim walk in Ireland that is approved by the Irish Camino Society. Recommended Celtic Camino routes include St. Declan's Way, St. Finbarr's Pilgrim Path, St. Kevin's Way (From Hollywood), and the Tóchar Phádraig. You may complete any 25km section on St Declan's Way. These paths, which were described earlier in this book, have a passport stamping system. This acts as convenient evidence of having completed the required walk. Other routes that the Irish Camino Society accepts are the Croagh Patrick Heritage Trail, Boyne Valley Camino, Bray Coastal Camino and the Kerry Camino.

Having completed the walk, you should bring or post the stamped pilgrim passport to the Camino Society information centre, at St James Street in Dublin. They will certify that you have walked a 25km route by issuing a Celtic Camino Compostela. You then recommence your pilgrim journey in A Coruña and walk the 75km to Santiago. Here, submit your stamped Pilgrim Passport for the A Corúna route along with your Celtic Camino Compostela and you will be granted a full Camino de Santiago Compostela.

Dún an geata
le do thoil

Please close
the gate

08 CROAGH PATRICK HERITAGE TRAIL
CO. MAYO

Overview. *Re-opened in 2009 and denoted by a circular blue, white and green logo*, this trail extends from the village of Balla in central Mayo, to Murrisk at the base of Croagh Patrick, which was the location of a 15th-century Augustinian friary. A highly varied trail, it passes through woodland and farmland while also traversing some raised bog. It utilises boreens and ancient pathways as it wends its way toward its destination on the shores of Clew Bay. The trail is at the beating heart of rural West Mayo; it includes many captivating heritage sites along the route and features other areas of great natural beauty. Completing this trail does not require an ascent to the summit of Croagh Patrick but ends instead at the main trailhead carpark for the mountain.

Suitability: This trail runs roughly east to west and is mainly at a low level. Walkers should, however, note that the route reaches a high point of 310 metres on the eastern foothills of Croagh Patrick. Services are available at Balla, Ballintubber, Aughagower and Murrisk.

Start: *Community Resource Centre, Balla.*

Finish: *Car park at Murrisk, which is situated 8kms to the west of Westport, on the coast road to Louisburgh.*

Time: *3 days.*

Total Distance: *60km.*

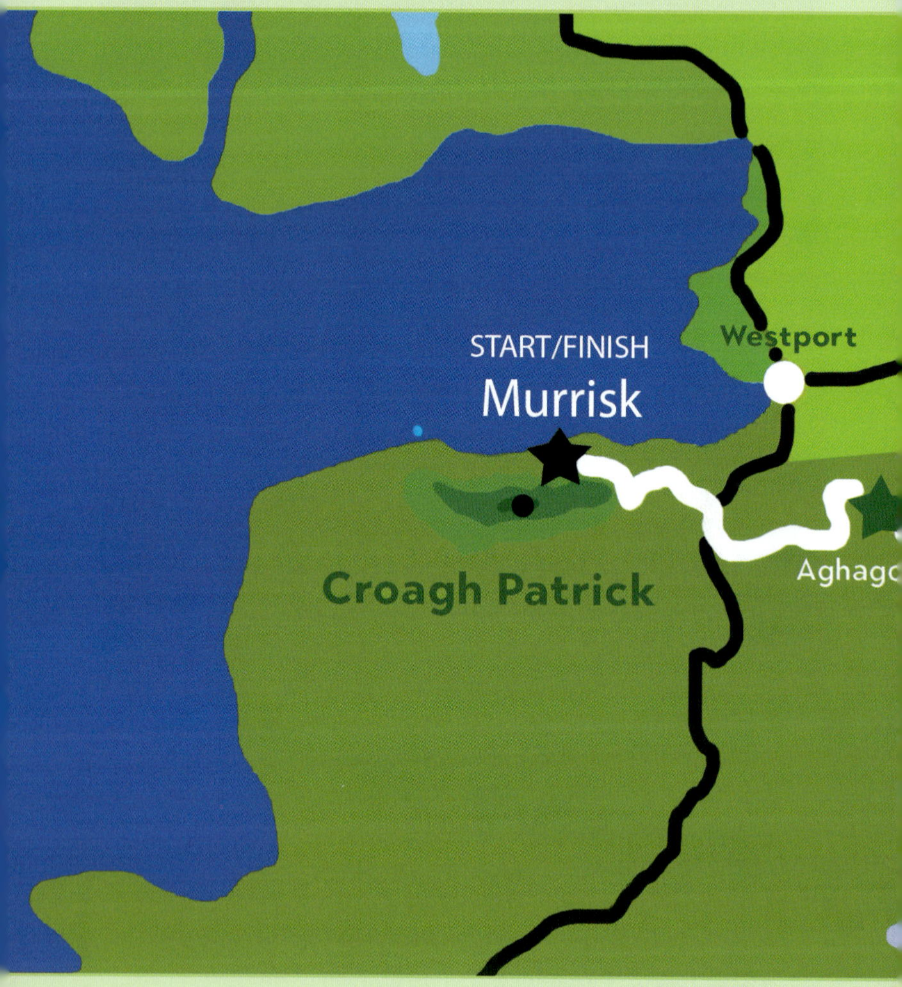
START/FINISH
Murrisk
Westport
Croagh Patrick
Aghagc

CROAGH PATRICK HERITAGE TRAIL
CO. MAYO

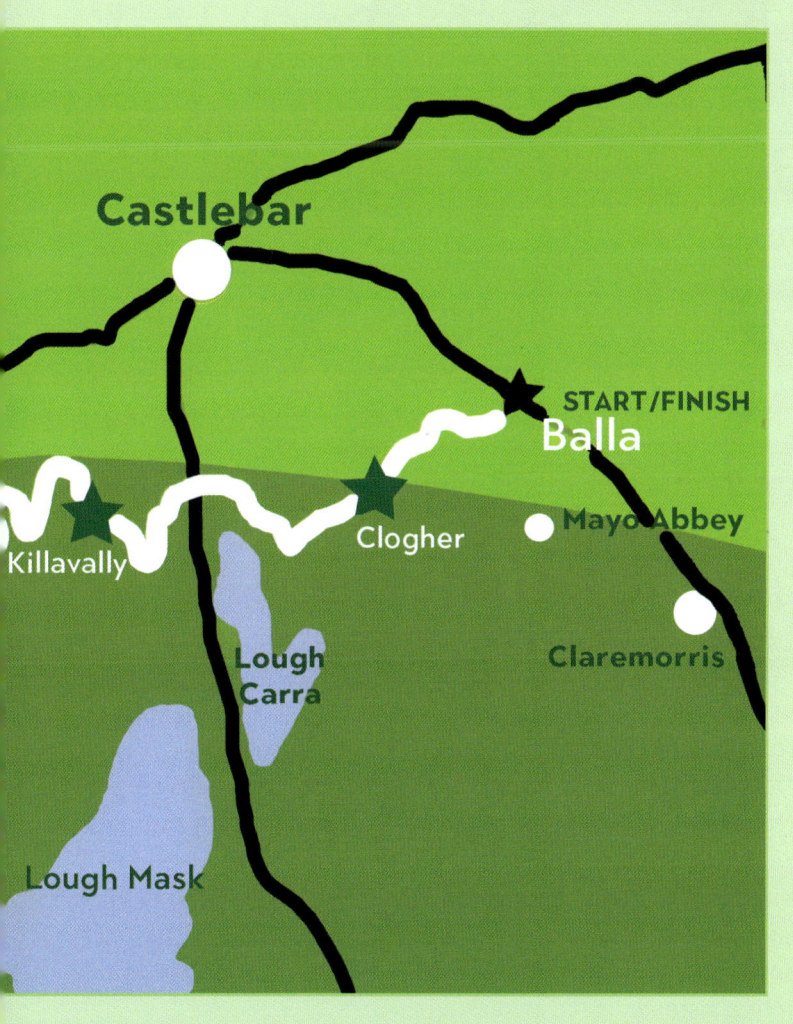

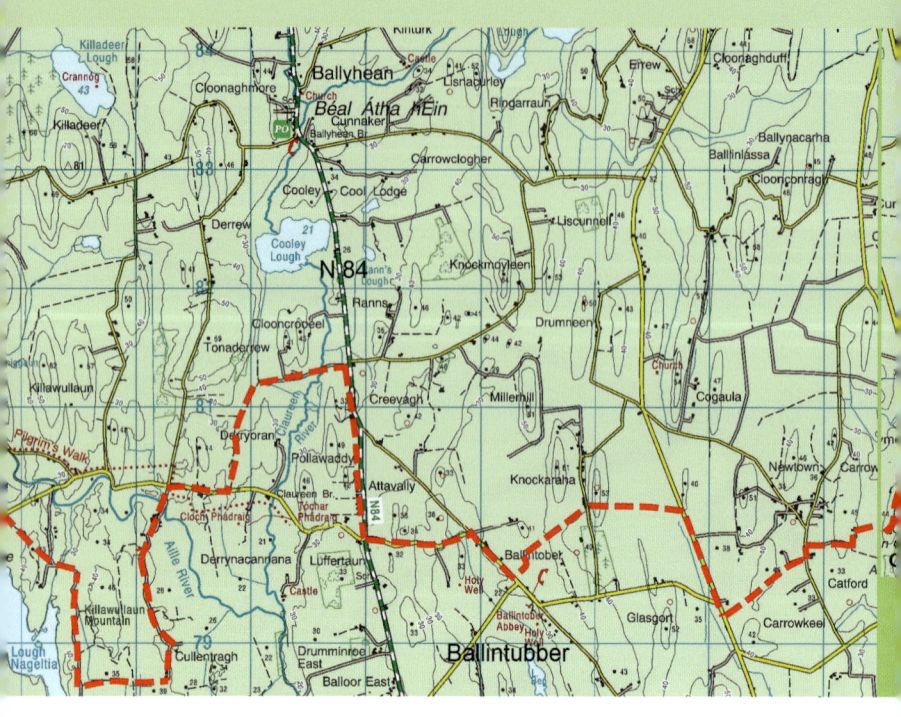

DAY 1
BALLA TO BALLINTUBBER
16KM

Your journey starts from Balla, the site of an early Christian monastic settlement founded by St Mochau in the 7th century. The first 17km stage is a relatively unchallenging outing to Ballintubber. Starting the walk, you will pass by a holy well, which is reputed to have been blessed by St Patrick in the year 441. It later developed into a significant pilgrimage site, until a Marian apparition at nearby Knock in 1879 diverted the faithful to this shrine instead.

Deeply rural lanes then convey you to the Claremorris to

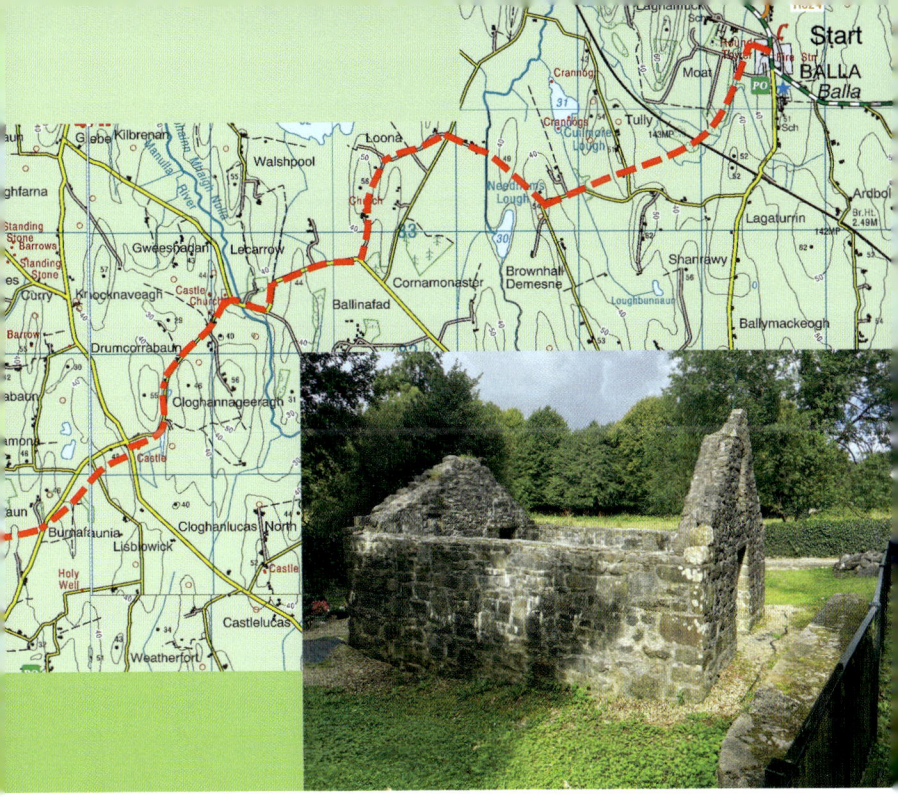

Castlebar railway line. Beyond, the route is mainly off-road through delightful field systems, with occasional excursions on quiet back roads. There are many echoes from the past, including the skeletal remains of Doonamona Castle, which was a stronghold of the powerful Burke family, who dominated Connaught up to the 16th century. Nearby is Tuffy's traditional Irish Pub, which was opened prior to the great Irish Famine in 1841.

The route then meanders about 400km north of the tiny hamlet of Clogher, before continuing mostly through fields and along country lanes to emerge onto a road beside Ballintubber Abey. This makes a good place to finish your day's walk and overnight since Corley's Pub, which lies directly opposite the Abbey, provides good quality food and a couple of nearby family homes offer overnight accommodation.

Balla monastic site

CROAGH PATRICK HERITAGE TRAIL HERITAGE TRAIL   117

DAY 2
BALLINTUBBER TO AUGHAGOWER
26KM

Beyond Ballintubber, the Heritage Trail initially joins the busy N84 for a short walk that offers the security of a wide shoulder and grass margin before swinging left onto a sylvan lane with a reassuring line of green down the middle. On the approach to Aughagower, the route meanders on and off road. On one occasion the Heritage Way coalesces with the route of the Tóchar Phádraig path for a short excursion through fields but then follows a more circuitous route. The varied terrain includes

Croagh Patrick Heritage Trail

118   GREAT IRISH PILGRIM JOURNEYS

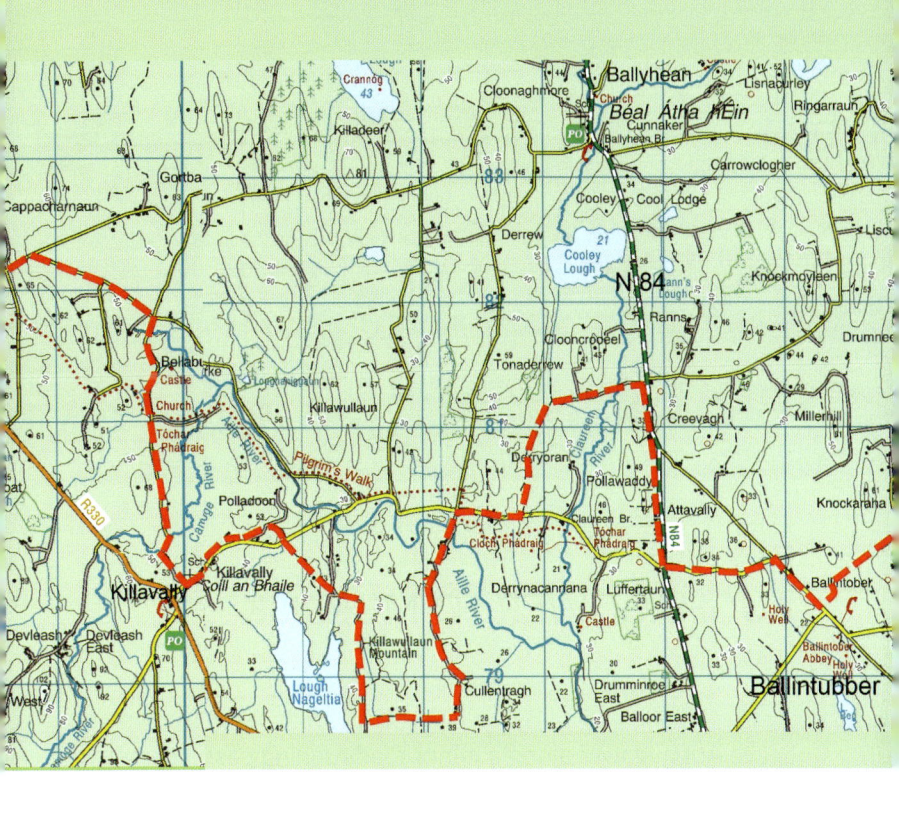

a 2km ramble through forestry, while you also pass through fields, along boreens and byroads. The approach to Aughagower is by way of a minor road from the south with your day finishing here with the opportunity of a pit stop in the atmospheric ambience of Scott's Bar.

Walkers should note that on the approach to Aughagower the Tóchar Phádraig is more direct and those under time pressure may be tempted to pay the €15 registration fee and walk the Tóchar from Ballintubber Abbey, which will take about 11km off your walk to Aughagower. It also means that if you are reasonably fit, you can complete your walk from Ballintubber in one day. It will require an extra day if you follow the Heritage Trail, but your reward is extra time meandering the peaceful Mayo countryside.

DAY 3
AUGHAGOWER TO MURRISK
18KM

Leave Aughagower along a minor road running past a cemetery and offering panoramic views of Croagh Patrick. You will now share the route with the Tóchar Phádraig pilgrim path for about 7km until you reach the Boheh Stone. The trail follows a leafy lane left to reach a minor road. From here the direction is to the right along tarred back roads for about 5km before following a rural lane to pass by the entrance for the Boheh Stone, which was described earlier as part of the Tóchar Phádraig walk. Here you part company with the Tóchar and continue along the lane to reach the N59.

There is a short section along this busy road before the trail goes left and follows a minor road. Almost immediately you go right and off-road through the natural splendour of Blackloon Wood and continue along a shaded path for almost 2km. Emerging from the trees, the direction is left followed by a right, and then through a farmyard before you clamber upwards along tarred byroads to coalesce for a time with the Western Way as this renowned walking route approaches Westport.

Both routes now swing left and continue ascending together along a stony track until the Heritage Trail swings right off the Western Way. The last section of your walk involves about 3km along rough tracks and across open mountainside. This area can be quite wet and rough underfoot but compensates by offering a great view over multi-islanded Clew Bay with the lordly Nephin Mountains beyond.

The Croagh Patrick Heritage Trail joins with the busy path ascending Croagh Patrick from Murrisk at a point just above a swing gate. At this stage, it is approximately 400 metres downhill to the right along a rough, eroded track and then a series of steps to where the Heritage Way finishes at Murrisk Carpark.

09 BOYNE VALLEY
CO. LOUTH

Overview: *This is a self-guided, 25km looped walk from Drogheda, which is one of the recommended routes for the Celtic Camino. The path goes through historic Drogheda, along the River Boyne and then continues through beautiful Townley Hall woods to reach Mellifont Abbey. It returns through the village of Tullyallen, and enters Drogheda along the memorable Boyneside Trail. The Celtic Camino Passports can be used to collect beautiful stamps created by local artists at stamping points along the route.*

Before setting out, it is best to download the detailed map of the entire route, which is available from caminosociety.ie

Suitability: *Easy outing along urban streets, minor roads, country lanes and woodland paths, with virtually no ascent.*

Start/Finish: *St Peter's Church, West St, Drogheda.*

Estimated Time: *6 hours (return).*

Distance: *25km.*

Mellifont Abbey. Oliver Gargan / Wikimedia ▶

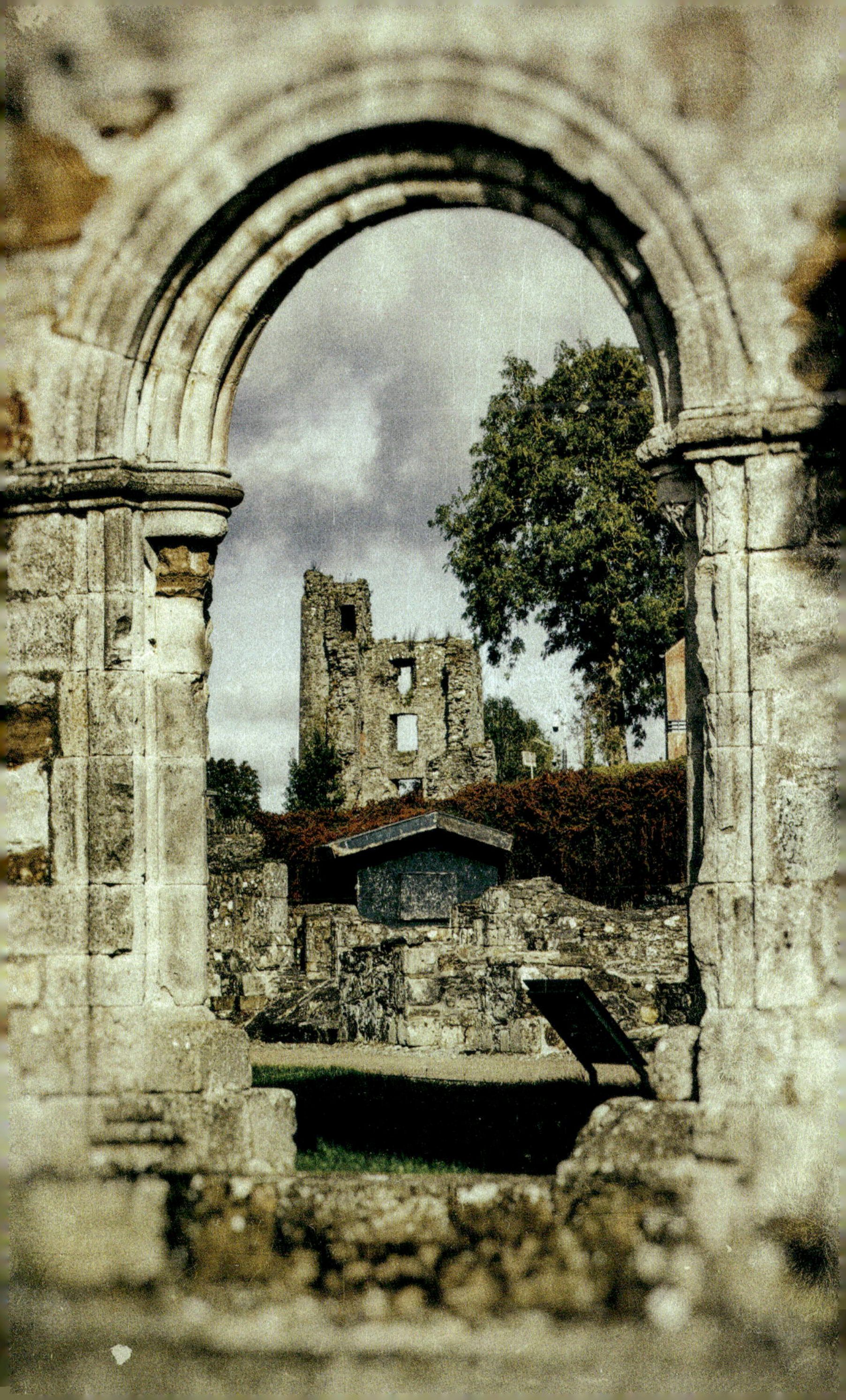

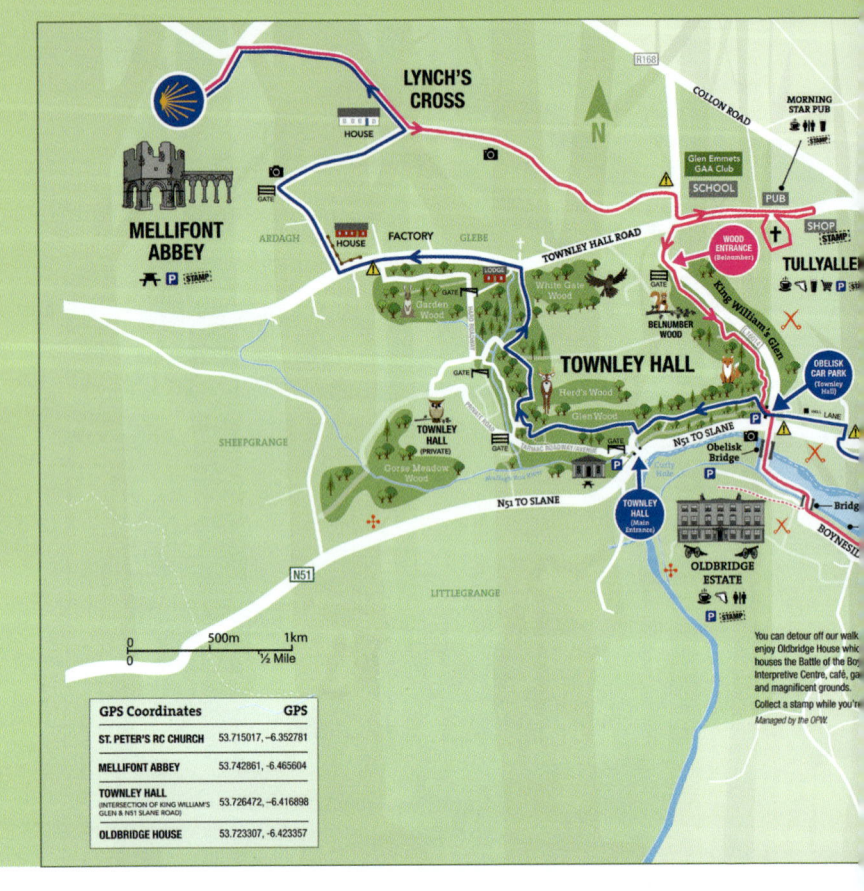

Founded in 1142, at the invitation of Ireland's St Malachy of Armagh, by monks from a French Abbey at Clairvaux, Mellifont was the first Cistercian house in Ireland. Its coming heralded the demise of the long-established Celtic monasteries such as nearby Monasterboice, which were then regarded as out of line with the doctrine of the Roman Church. The highly formalised Cistercian Rule was now the spirit of the age and quickly spread nationwide like a prairie fire. During this period, there was strong historical evidence that pilgrims travelled long distances to Drogheda before embarking for A Coruña in Spain and then continuing to Santiago.

BOYNE VALLEY CAMINO

www.boynevalleycamino.ie

    To commemorate this, the ancient route linking Mellifont with the medieval port of Drogheda has recently been revived, with the trailhead located outside St Peter's Church on West Street. Here the route goes west on West Street then down a lane leading to the banks of the River Boyne. Gaining a busy junction at an Aldi Store, the way is uphill and then left along a quiet lane leading beneath the M1 Motorway and across the busy Drogheda to Slane Road.

    Following a walkway paralleling this road, you enter a wood where an enclosed path leads to the roadway serving the Townley Estate. Continue to the entrance gate for Townley Hall. The route

BOYNE VALLEY   125

goes right here, making its way through serene woodlands with occasional tantalising glimpses of the great house, which is regarded as one of Ireland's finest examples of classic Georgian architecture.

A tarmaced private road and then another lane now handrails you to the busy Townley Hall Road, where the way is left. After about a kilometre, you are back on hushed byroads that beckon left at Lynch's Cross and soon after down the cul-de-sac road leading to Mellifont Abbey.

For your return journey, retrace your steps to Lynch's Cross, but continue straight on for 1.6kms to a T-Junction at Tullyallen School. Go right here and almost immediately left. Then continue into Tullyallen village to have your passport stamped in the local supermarket or in the Morning Star pub. Retrace your steps to the crossroads at Tullyallen School and go left here. Soon afterward, the arrows lead off-road through a wood known locally as King Williams Glen, so named because it was here that William of Orange made camp prior to the Battle of the Boyne.

Once beyond the trees, cross the busy N51 and continue straight ahead over the well-known Obelisk Bridge, where a monument to King William's victory once stood. The monument was destroyed by explosives soon after Irish Independence and all that now remains is the bridge.

Next, it is across the Boyne Canal before accessing the Boyneside Trail on your left. Follow this splendid walk as it leads you beneath the great edifice of the Mary McAleese Bridge and then continues first along a footpath and then off-road for another 2kms of waterside walking to regain Drogheda. Go under the Bridge of Peace before crossing St Dominic's Pedestrian Bridge and then continue up Dominic Street. Go right at a T-Junction and this will return you to St Peter's Church.

ST OLIVER PLUNKETT

Born in Co. Meath in 1629, Plunkett studied for the priesthood in Rome, at a time when Catholic seminaries were banned in Ireland, and was ordained in 1654. After some years of teaching and ministering in Rome, he was appointed Archbishop of Armagh in 1669.

Back in Ireland, he set about reorganising the Church and building schools. In 1678, the so-called Popish Plot concocted in England by clergyman Titus Oates alleged that members of the Catholic Church were conspiring to assassinate King Charles II. This led to a wave of anti-Catholicism that forced Plunkett into hiding. He was finally arrested in December 1679 and charged with plotting a French invasion of Ireland. Knowing he would never be convicted in Dublin the British authorities moved his trial to London and there he was found guilty of high treason. In June 1681 he was condemned to be hanged, drawn and quartered. His head was later returned to Ireland and now rests in a reliquary within St Peter's Church, Drogheda, which is the startpoint for the Boyne Valley Camino.

10 BRAY COASTAL CAMINO
DUBLIN & WICKLOW

Overview: *Commemorating pilgrims who came to Dublin and then sailed on to walk the Camino, this is a journey from Bray that finishes at St James Church, Dublin, so it is almost entirely within an urban setting. This may seem initially off-putting, but it shouldn't really. This is a wonderfully varied walk with much that is fascinating along the way while offering plenty of memorable sea views. In general, you will be walking with the Irish Sea and later the River Liffey never far to your right, but often not visible. Since you are walking through an urban space, services are plentiful along the route.*

You can get your passport stamped at different locations, and by finishing the coastal route, you are entitled to receive a Celtic Camino Compostela from the St James Church office of the Irish Camino Society. At the time of writing the stamping locations for your passport were: St. James's Church, Crinken; The James Joyce Tower,

Sandycove; Dublin Tourist Information Centre, Queens Rd, Dun Laoghaire; Christ Church Cathedral, Dublin; St. James's Church, James's Street, Dublin.

Suitability: *The Bray Coastal Camino is a rather lengthy walk to complete in one day. Those with the sufficient time may prefer to complete it over a more leisurely 2 or perhaps 3 days. Walkers should also note the walk is not waymarked. A comprehensive turn-by-turn account of the route is, however, available within the Bray Celtic Camino brochure which can be downloaded from the website of the Irish Camino Society at, www.caminosociety.ie*

Getting there: *Your walk begins from the large town of Bray, which is easily accessible from Dublin using the Dart commuter rail line. This train journey takes about 45 minutes.*

Start: *The Camino waymarker (Mouteira) outside Finnbees Restaurant, on the seafront at Bray, where you can obtain the first stamp for your pilgrim passport.*

Finish: *Church of St. James, James St, Dublin.*

Estimated Time: *7 hours.*

Distance: *30km.*

Bray harbour

Start by walking north along the seafront to Bray Harbour. Cross a bridge, veer left and away from the coast to follow the Dargle Walkway. Go right and follow Castle Street, the Dublin Road and then the road signed Shankill at Wilford Roundabout. The second stamping station is at Crinken Evangelical Church. This is located on your right, with the stamper in a box on the Church's north wall. Then it is on through leafy Shanganagh Park, where a second stone mouteira gives welcome evidence, that you are still on the route. Beyond Shangangh, it is past Shankill Tennis Club and along Corbawn Drive, Corbawn Avenue and Seafield to regain the coast. One of the nicest sections of the route now follows as you tag a lovely pathway paralleling the coastline before descending onto the soft sands of Killiney Beach.

Then, it is inland along Station Road and Vico Road. One of the most exclusive addresses in Dublin, Vico Road is home to Bono, Enya and The Edge. Coliemore Road follows and another sea view at Coliemore Harbour. Inland again on Convent Road and

ST JAMES'S CHURCH

St. James's Church,
James's Street,
Dublin 8
The Church Sacristy
Mon-Fri 8:30am
to 11:45am all year

Camino Society
Information Centre
Thurs-Sat
10:30am to 15:30pm
March to mid-October

DUBLIN CITY

RINGSEND

SANDYMOUNT

BOOTERSTOWN
BLACKROCK

DÚN LAOGHAIRE

SANDYCOVE
DALKEY

KILLINEY
KILLINEY HILL

SHANKILL
CRINKEN CHURCH

BRAY

County Dublin

County Wicklow

CAMINO SOCIETY
IRELAND

BRAY COASTAL CAMINO   131

Harbour Road until you reach Bullock Harbour and soon after the famous Forty-Foot bathing place and James Joyce Tower. Originally an exclusively male bathing place, it was the scene of a feminist protest about this fact in 1974. As a result, it is now open to both sexes and makes a nice place to bathe your feet on a warm day.

The nearby Martello Tower houses a museum devoted to the life and works of James Joyce, who used it as the setting for the first chapter of his great work, Ulysses. You can get your passport stamped inside the Museum.

Pass Sandycove Beach and continue along the Victorian elegance of the Dún Laoghaire seafront. Get another passport stamp at the tourist office opposite the Royal St George Yacht Club before following the coastal path to Seapoint Martello Tower.

Next, go by Blackrock Dart Station, enter Blackrock Park and continue onto Rock Road. Continue past Booterstown Nature Reserve to Merrion Gates. Go right to follow Strand Road and Irishtown Road to cross over the River Dodder, where steps now convey you onto South Dock Road. Go left over the lock gates of the Grand Canal and continue along Hanover Quay, which is located on the north side of Grand Canal Dock. From here the Grand Canal, which took 47 years to construct, links Dublin to the River Shannon. Once an important commercial link, it is now the exclusive playground of recreationalists.

A right on Benson Street and then left along the River Liffey Quays leads to the Séan O'Casey Bridge. Cross this to North Quays and continue past the Custom House – a Palladian-style building designed by the English architect James Gandon, who also designed the Dublin Four Courts and King's Inns. The building was burned in 1921 during the Irish War of Independence but was later fully restored.

Return to the South Quays over Butt Bridge and walk directly

CHRISTCHURCH CATHEDRAL

Located at the heart of Viking Dublin but remaining an island of peace surrounded by frenetic traffic, Christchurch Cathedral is now the seat of the Church of Ireland Archbishop of Dublin. Initially constructed in 1030 by the Norse King of the City, it was hugely extended and remodelled by the Normans following their invasion of Ireland. Renowned for its magnificent architectural features and wonderful floor tiles, Christchurch houses the tomb of Strongbow, leader of the Norman invaders, who captured Dublin in 1170. Also housed in the Cathedral is a reliquary containing the heart of St Laurence O'Toole who was the Archbishop of Dublin at the time of the Normal invasion and later became renowned as a miracle worker. The Cathedral became Anglican at the time of the English Reformation, but to this day the Pope claims Christchurch as the rightful seat of the Roman Catholic Archbishop of Dublin.

south to reach the wall of Trinity College, which was founded in 1592 and is Ireland's oldest university. With the Trinity Walls on your left, continue to College Green. Go up Dame Street to reach Christchurch Cathedral, which lies at the medieval heart of old Dublin and is the seat of the Anglican Archbishop of Dublin and Glendalough. Having stamped your passport, continue directly on by High Street, Thomas Street and James Street to finish at St James Church, which is on the left-hand side opposite Guinness.

11 KERRY CAMINO
CO. KERRY

Overview: The Kerry Camino follows a section of the famous Dingle Way between Tralee and Dingle that most walkers complete in 3 days. It commemorates the fact that pilgrims past would have walked to St. James' Church in Dingle, which was originally built by Spanish merchants who dedicated it to the patron saint of Spain. Many of these pilgrims would then have embarked on a ship to A Coruña as part of their spiritual journey to visit the tomb of St. James in Santiago.

Along the way, you will find the route is well-marked with arrows for the Dingle Way and larger signs indicating the Kerry Camino.

Start: St. John's Church, which is located in the town centre of Tralee, Co. Kerry.

Finish: Church of St. James, Dingle.

Distance: 58km.

Logbook: On the Kerry Camino, walkers can use a logbook and the stamping stations along the route to *mark their progress. Logbooks are available for free from the tourist offices in Tralee and Dingle. Completion certificates are issued by the tourist offices on the production of a fully stamped passport.*

A minimum of 8 stamps on a logbook is required to receive a Walk Certificate for the Kerry Camino. Certificates of completion can be collected at Dingle or Tralee Tourist Offices by producing a logbook with 8 stamps. Stamping stations are located in business premises at all the villages and also at rest benches along the route. For further information on the route and location of the stamping stations, visit, kerrycamino.com.

Hedge-lined path on the Kerry Camino

DAY 1
TRALEE TO CAMP
21KM

Start: *St. John's Church, Tralee, Co. Kerry.*

Finish: *Camp.*

Estimated Time: *6.5 hours.*

Distance: *21km.*

Start by crossing the town park to Princes Street where a left turn leads to a busy roundabout. Go right and follow the right bank of the Tralee Canal to a bridge leading towards Blennerville Windmill. At this point, the Dingle Way branches away from the North Kerry Way and crosses the canal to enter Blennerville village.

The Way follows the main N86 road to Dingle for a short distance before taking the second left and following some quieter country roads that gradually ascend the eastern flanks of the Slieve Mish Mountains. After around 3km, the trail reaches Tonavane and gains open mountainside.

The route now moves west, paralleling the busy N86 Dingle/Tralee main road with the mighty Slieve Mish towering to your left. The underfoot conditions are rough here and it can also become wet and boggy in places, so watch your step. Towards the end of this section, the trail descends closer to the main road before segueing onto a hedge-lined path, which was the main Tralee-Dingle Road in olden times. The ruins of Killelton Oratory, which was built by St Eltan in the 10th century, can be explored near the trail. Beyond, several more stiles are crossed to finally reach a tarmac road.

The last section of the walk bears left and rises briefly before meeting a minor road. It then descends to the Finglas River and crosses this using stepping stones before continuing to where the Dingle Way signs point in 3 directions. Go right here for about 1km to reach Camp Village at Ashes Pub, which is conveniently located near a large filling station and shop.

Note: *If the water levels make crossing the stepping stones on the Finglas River problematic, you should retrace your steps and go left and then left again along the N86 to reach Camp.*

KERRY CAMINO

Path on the Kerry Camino

DAY 2
CAMP TO ANNASCAUL
18KM

Start: Camp.
Finish: Annascaul.
Estimated Time: 6 hours.
Distance: 18km.

Rejoining the trail to the west of the Finglas River crossing, the Dingle Way follows a linear south-westerly direction for 2km, while gradually ascending with views of Caherconree Mountain and the impressive megalithic fort of Caherconree.

The route crosses between the peaks of Corrin and Knockbrack before swinging left through a gateway on a magnificent track leading for about 4km through serene, open moorland with expansive mountain views in all directions. Beyond, the trail gradually descends for 2km, through woodland and later pasture land before reaching a minor public road where the way is left. The Kerry Camino briefly follows the course of this road until it crosses the Emlagh River, whereupon it dives right onto a rough track. This gradually swings around to the west and reveals a spectacular view of Inch Beach. It was here that scenes from Ryan's Daughter were filmed at the end of the 1960s by renowned British filmmaker, David Leen. Now one of Ireland's most popular and scenic beaches, it offers comprehensive facilities including a café, a shop and a pub that serves food. It may be worth taking a break here by following a road downhill to the left for a short distance to reach the beach.

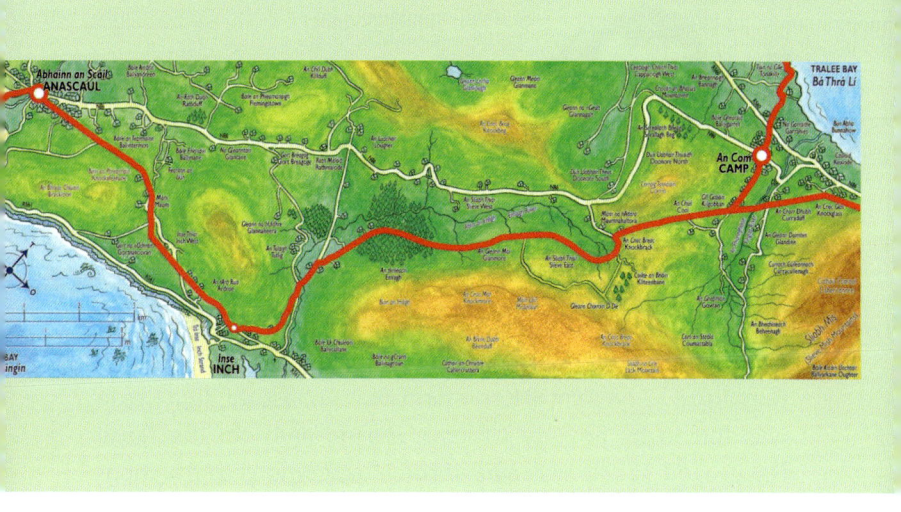

The Way now climbs along a rough track before descending to a byroad. From here it meanders on and offroad again as it ascends to reach Maum at a height of 180m. Passing close by Knockafeehane Mountain, your immediate reward is a magnificent view of Lough Anascaul, which is situated in a dramatic glacial valley of the Slieve Mish Mountains. Beyond, take the left option at a fork in the road and then continue the final 2km on tarmac to reach the heart of Annascaul village.

TOM CREAN, ANTARCTIC EXPLORER

Born in 1877 on a small Kerry farm near Annascaul, Tom Crean was forced by poverty to leave Ireland and join the Royal Navy, aged 15. He was part of three expeditions to the then-unexplored Antarctic continent. Two of these were led by the ill-fated Robert Falcon Scott, while Crean's final expedition was under the leadership of Ernest Shackleton.

During this expedition, Shackleton's ship, the Endurance, became trapped in ice and sank. The crew then made their way across the ice to Elephant Island off the coast of Antarctica. From here, Shackleton, Crean, and a few other crew members, in an incredible display of seamanship, sailed in a tiny boat for 1,300km to South Georgia, the nearest inhabited island. Arriving in South Georgia, Crean and his companions were obliged to cross the island's frozen mountains to raise the alarm. They succeeded, and this resulted in the entire crew of the Endurance being rescued from Elephant Island, without a single loss of life.

When Tom Crean retired from the Navy in 1920, he returned home to Annascaul and opened a pub called The South Pole Inn. A visit to this pub is well worthwhile for the fine collection of memorabilia from Crean's life. Across the road, there is a statue of the Kerry-born explorer by the Irish American sculptor Jerome Connor who was also born in Annascaul.

DAY 3
ANNASCAUL TO DINGLE
19KM

Start: *Anascaul village.*

Finish: *St James' Church.*

Estimated Time: *5 hours.*

Distance: *19km.*

Departing Annascaul, the Dingle Way briefly joins the main Tralee-Dingle Road before swinging left onto the R561 Killarney Road and then right onto the much quieter Gurteen Road. This twists and turns for over 4km before finally descending to sea level beside the ruin of the 16th-century Minard Castle. This lovely beach offers a magnificent vista across Dingle Bay to the mountains of the Iveragh Peninsula.

Minard is a mid-16th century castle built by the Fitzgerald's, who held the title Knights of Kerry. All occupants of the castle were killed and the structural damage done made the building uninhabitable when Oliver Cromwell's forces attacked it in the mid-16th century.

Leaving the shoreline, go left on tarmac and soon after go right as the Dingle Way ascends a narrow path to follow a small boreen and a minor road in a north-westerly direction. The Way ascends for a bit before swinging left along a lane and continuing to a T-Junction. Turn right and ascend past Aglish Cemetery. Beyond, go right and then left at a T-junction. Follow this minor road as it descends for 2km before swinging right to gain the tiny settlement of Lispole just opposite O'Cathain's (Keane's) Shop, where you may wish to top up your supplies. The name of the shop is a reminder that you are now entering the Gaeltacht (Irish-speaking) area of West Kerry. Don't worry about your ability to communicate, however, everyone in the area also speaks English.

Having crossed the main N86, the trail ascends north from Lispole on a minor road for about 1km before swinging left for about 1.5km. Here arrows point right into a field and soon after indicate left along a rural lane. For the next 5km or so the route leads through working farms. First, the Way goes left along a lane and through rough pasture. This leads to a succession of farm tracks with occasional short excursions on tarmac roads. Eventually, you will cross a bridge over the Garfinny River to reach a metalled roadway. Follow this to the left past a swing gateway to reach the Conor Pass Road (R60). Go directly across and onto a gravel lane that descends to join Spa Road and then continues to descend for 1km to reach Dingle. Keep straight ahead to reach Dingle Main Street and go right here to complete your pilgrim journey at the Church of St James on your right.

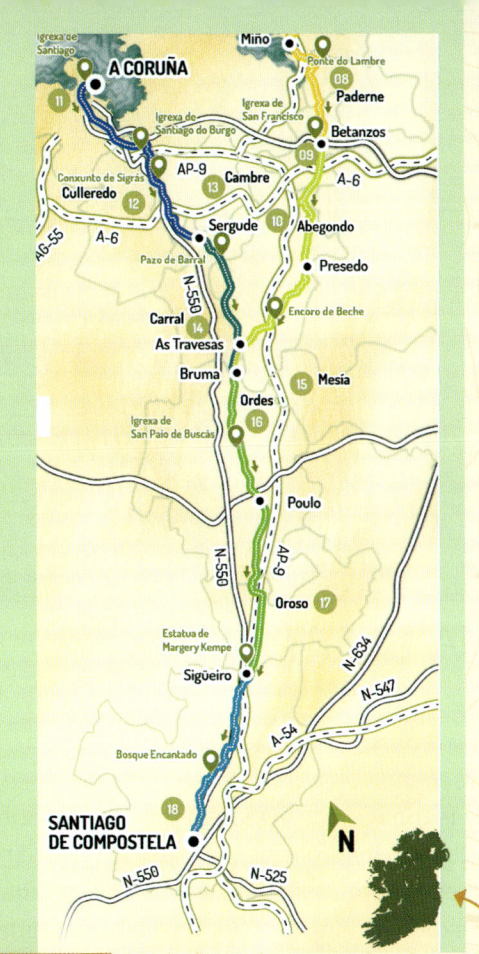

12 A CORUÑA TO SANTIAGO
SPAIN

Start: *The Church of Santiago, A Coruña.*

Finish: *Cathedral of Santiago, Santiago.*

Distance: *75km.*

DAY 1

A CORUÑA **TO SERGUDE**
20KM

The penitential section of the day comes at the beginning of the 20km walk. This is the 10k or so through the city and suburbs of A Coruña with the waymarkers for the Camino often difficult to find, or sometimes absent, amid the jumble of other urban signs. You shouldn't experience too many navigational difficulties, however, if you remember the direction is generally south and the sea should be on you left when visible. After about 4km you begin climbing for 1km to cross the high point of Eiris. From here, the route descends to Ria O Burgo and then continues along the waterside for about 5km. At O Burgo Bridge, the Camino Inglés leaves the waterside and ascends to Almerias before continuing downhill to cross over the A6 Autoroute and reach the Galician countryside, which generally becomes less populated the further you walk from *A Coruña*. Quiet back roads and occasional woodland paths now convey you very pleasantly to your day's end at Hostel Peregrinos de Sergude-Carral.

Torre de Hércules, La Coruña. Diego Delso / Wikimedia

RED HUGH O'DONNELL

Soon after the defeat of the Gaelic chieftains at the Battle of Kinsale in 1601, Red Hugh O'Donnell sailed to A Coruña with a promise to his supporters that he would return to Ireland with a large army. After following the well-trodden penitential route to Santiago de Compostela, he was lavishly welcomed as an honoured guest and enemy of England by the archbishop and was quartered in the episcopal palace.

With his sagging self-confidence likely restored, he travelled on to the Spanish royal court at Valladolid to request further help from Philip III of Spain, who apparently committed himself to a second invasion of Ireland. Time went by, however, and O'Donnell did not receive any favourable response from Philip who had become short of money and after recent failures was, perhaps, wary of further expensive expeditions against the English.

In the end, Hugh never made it back to Ireland. Impatient for action, he set out again for Valladolid to try a second time at persuading Philip but died unexpectedly en route at Simincas Castle on September 10, 1602.

DAY 2
SERGUDE TO HOSPITAL DE BRUMA
13KM

A short but challenging 13km route today. Immediately it is downhill to the right before going right and then left along a rural lane which soon segues into a pleasant track. Continue along peaceful rural lanes, and a forest path for a time before returning to paved roads with the route now climbing steadily. Entering the small settlement of Saradons, you will doubtless be glad to discover a café bar. Beyond, the route begins ascending more steeply before levelling out as it reaches a plateau where the elevation reaches almost 500m. After another short off-road excursion, the busier Camino Ingles coming from Ferrol joins from your left. Just beyond the meeting point, there is a café bar which makes a nice break as you have now completed 10km of your day's walk.

You are now likely to have more chance encounters with other pilgrims as you continue past a power station before swinging off the road through woodland and then regaining the highway and turning right to reach Bruma. This tiny settlement, which has provided hospitality to pilgrims since 1175, offers modern hostel accommodation and a nice café.

DAY 3
HOSPITAL DE BRUMA TO SIQUEIRO
25KM

Today, is an easier stage which involves a descent of almost 300m. The route runs almost directly south through green farmland and passing the small villages of Seixo and Cabeza de Lopo. Just beyond the tiny settlement of Carballira, the Camino goes off-road through woodland before reaching A Rua which has a nice place for lunch titled Café Bar Nova. Then it is on through the rural village of O Outeiro to Calle which also boasts a café bar. Beyond this, the trail meanders along several quiet roads with one delightful diversion along a shaded woodland track. The next 4kms are beside a busy autostrada. Eventually, the path abandons the autostrada and diverts along pleasant rural lanes leading to the suburbs of Siqueiro. Now it is just a question of following the waymarkers into Siqueiro.

Hospital de Bruma. Miguel Branco / Wikimedia

CORUÑA TO SANTIAGO

SANTIAGO DE COMPOSTELA

All Camino routes finish at the great square in front of Santiago Cathedral, which is known as the Praza do Obradoiro. Tradition holds that the remains of the apostle James, who had preached in Spain, were, after his death, taken from Jerusalem to Galicia for burial. The location of the grave became lost in the mists of time and was only re-discovered in the 9th century. It was then that the light of a shimmering star guided a shepherd named Pelagius to the burial site in Santiago de Compostela, where the Santiago Cathedral stands today. Now a UNESCO World Heritage Site, Santiago is a beautifully compact city worth visiting in its own right. It has a long tradition of links to Ireland. With Catholics unable to study in Ireland because of penal laws, an Irish College was set up in Santiago in 1605. The College continued to prepare Irishmen for the priesthood until the Irish Penal Laws were relaxed at the end of the 18th century and the National Seminary at Maynooth was established.

DAY 4
SIGUEIRO TO SANTIAGO
17KM

Your pilgrim journey now concludes with a relatively short 16.5km walk to Santiago Cathedral that involves 3 moderate level ascents with the N550 main road never far away. Leave Siqueiro by crossing a bridge over the River Tambre and then following the N550 main road as the route rises gently. Go right to meander along quiet public roads and occasional tracks that continue ascending. After crossing the Ap 9 Autostrada, walk beside it for a short time before going right and away from the road. Continue along quiet back roads until reaching a school, where you move off-road and into what has become known as the enchanted forest. Emerging from the trees, you are now in the outskirts of Santiago, where you pass through an industrial estate. All that remains is to follow the arrows into the old town to Santiago Cathedral and then go the short distance to get your passport stamped at the nearby Pilgrims Office.

◀ Cathedral de Santiago de Compostela.
Luis Miguel Bugallo Sánchez / Wikimedia

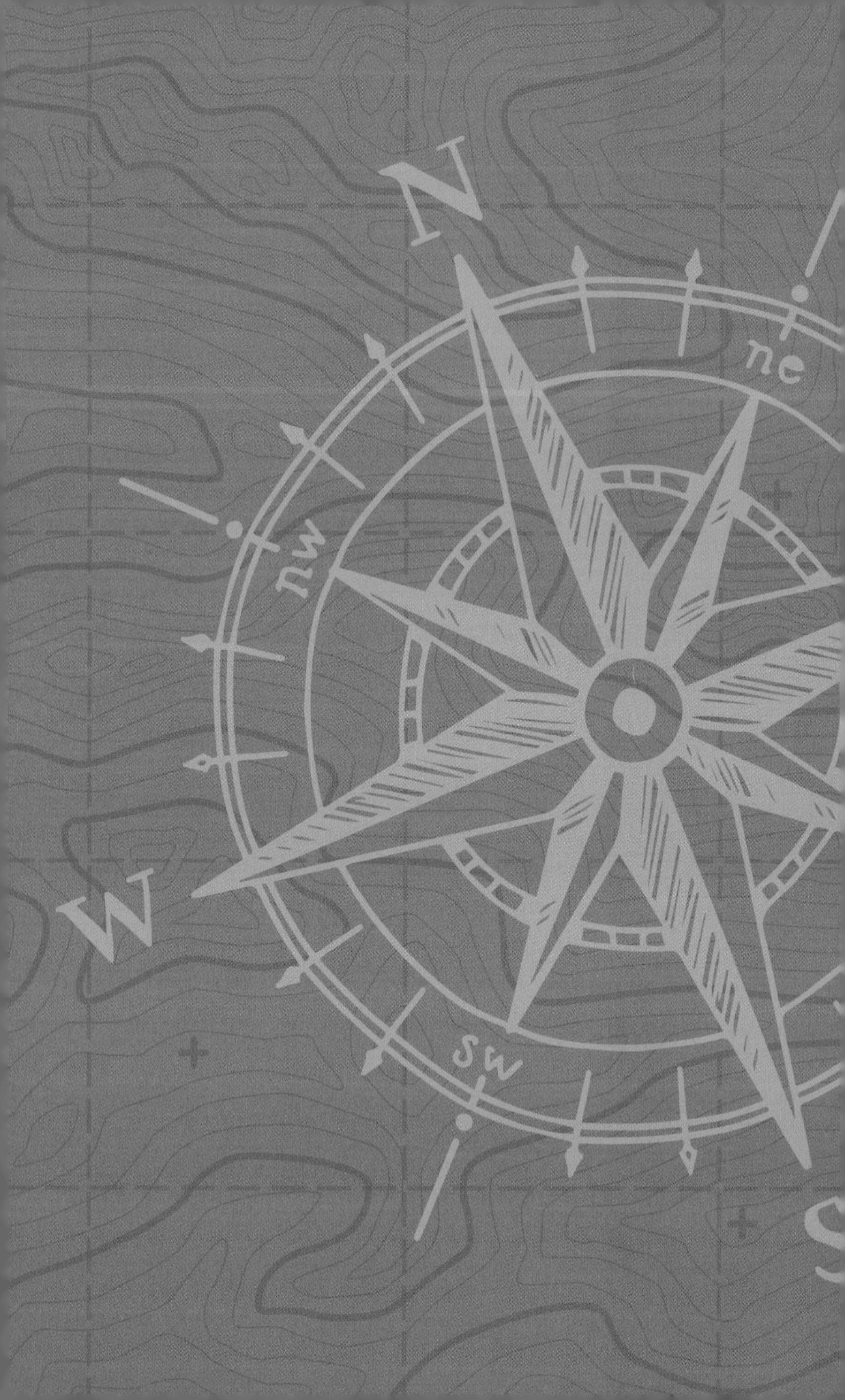
N
ne
nw
W
sw

ST PATRICK'S WAY

13 ST PATRICK'S WAY ARMAGH TO DOWNPATRICK

Overview: *Officially opened in 2015, St Patricks Way is a fully signposted route beginning from Navan Fort, Co. Armagh. It was here that Patrick reputedly healed a local chieftain named Daire, who, in gratitude, donated the site to build a hilltop church where Armagh City is now located. The route ends nearby his burial place in Downpatrick, Co. Down. The path offers some of the best and most varied scenery in Northern Ireland and includes 2 days of rambling among the splendid Mourne Mountains on fully waymarked walking trails.*

It is important for walkers undertaking the route to remember that shopping facilities are only available in the larger urban centres: Armagh, Tandragee, Newry, Rostrevor, Newcastle, Dundrum and Downpatrick, while there are convenience stores at Poyntzpass and Ballykinler. Pack your supplies with this in mind. Accommodation may also be difficult to find, particularly around Tandragee and Ballykinler, while you will need a pickup at the end of your walk from Rostrevor to the Spelga Pass.

Start: *Navan Fort, Co. Armagh. This is located about two miles west from Armagh City on the A28 main road to Caledon.*

Finish: *St Patrick's Centre, Downpatrick, Co. Down.*

Time: *6 to 8 days.*

Total Distance: *88 miles (141km).*

ST PATRICK

From his own words, we know Patrick was the son of a wealthy Christian living in Britain. Aged 16, he was captured by Irish raiders as the terminally weakened Roman Empire was unable to protect its borders and then he was sold to slavery in Ireland. During this period, he became increasingly religious and turned to long periods of prayer. After six years, he experienced a religious epiphany while tending flocks and believed God was calling him home. Motivated to escape, he found a ship that conveyed him away from Ireland and eventually he reached home after many adventures. Later, he studied Christianity and following an apparition, which suggested the Irish people were calling him back, he returned to Ireland as a bishop and converted the island to the new faith.

It is, of course, almost inconceivable that Patrick came to an island that had not previously been exposed to the Christian faith. The Roman Empire had, after all, been Christianised by Emperor Constantine more than a century before his arrival and Ireland had strong trade links with Britain and the Continent. Even though Patrick is unlikely to have been the sole evangeliser of Ireland, no other individual has influenced Irish lives so profoundly. Celebrated in more countries than any other, his feast day has morphed into an international event that involves the greening of hundreds of the world's most iconic locations. In recent years it has evolved into a global behemoth, and an international goodwill fest for Ireland of almost inestimable value.

ST PATRICK'S WAY

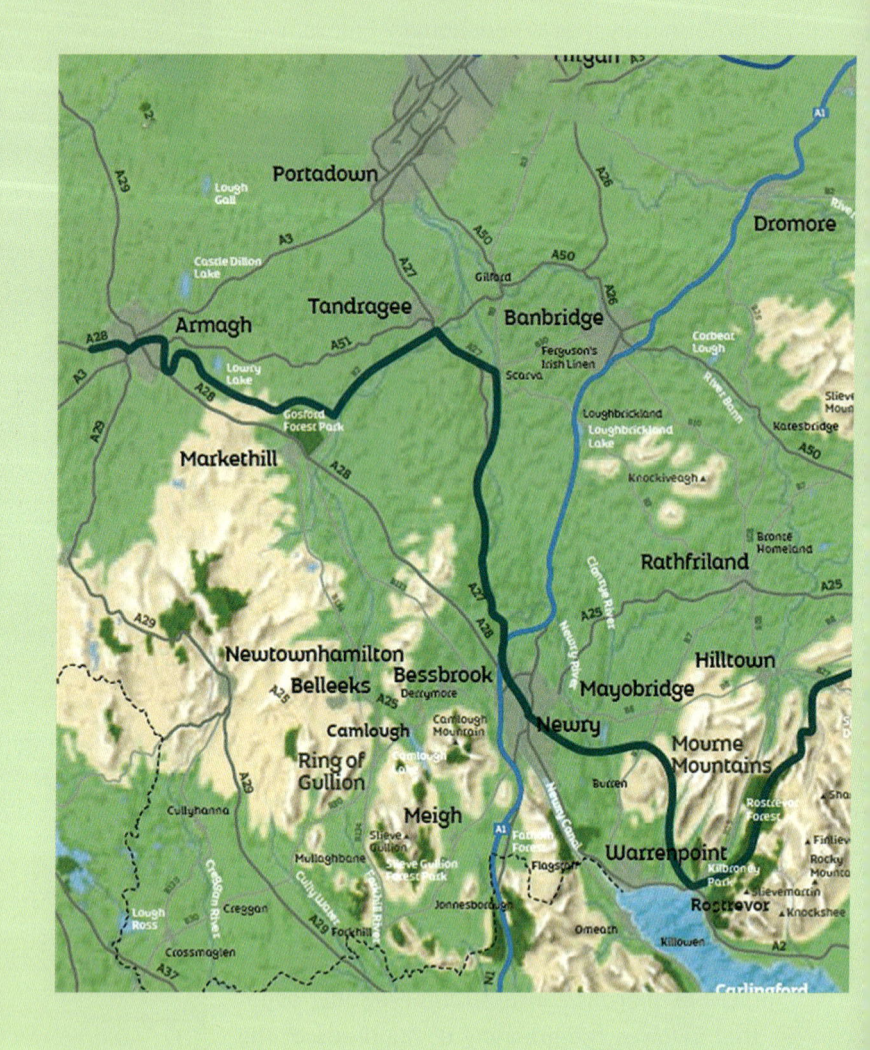

ARMAGH TO DOWN

ST PATRICK'S WAY 155

INTRODUCTION

The Irish Annals relate that, when close to death, Patrick was told by an angel to leave Armagh and return to his original Irish landing place at Saul, Co. Down. This was the location where he arrived to Ireland on his evangelical journey in 432. Having come full circle, he is reputed to have died here on March 17th, 461. The angel then returned and decreed Patrick's body be placed on an ox cart and buried where the oxen stopped. This was in Downpatrick at a location that today is beside the magnificent Down Cathedral. It makes a fitting endpoint for a Patrician journey and is the tradition that underlies St Patrick's Way linking Armagh with Downpatrick.

DAY 1
NAVAN FORT TO ARMAGH CITY
4KM

Your journey begins at Navan Fort, Co. Armagh, the ancient seat of the Kings of Ulster and one of Ireland's most important archaeological sites. First, get your passport stamped in the Navan Fort Visitor Centre and then make your way north to the start point at nearby Navan Fort. Continue east along Navan Fort Road for about 1.5km. Go left along Ballycummy Road and then right along Cathedral Road to gain Armagh city outskirts.

This is where Saint Patrick established the seat of Christianity in Ireland and the city grew around his church. Since your walk today is a short one, there should be plenty of time to explore

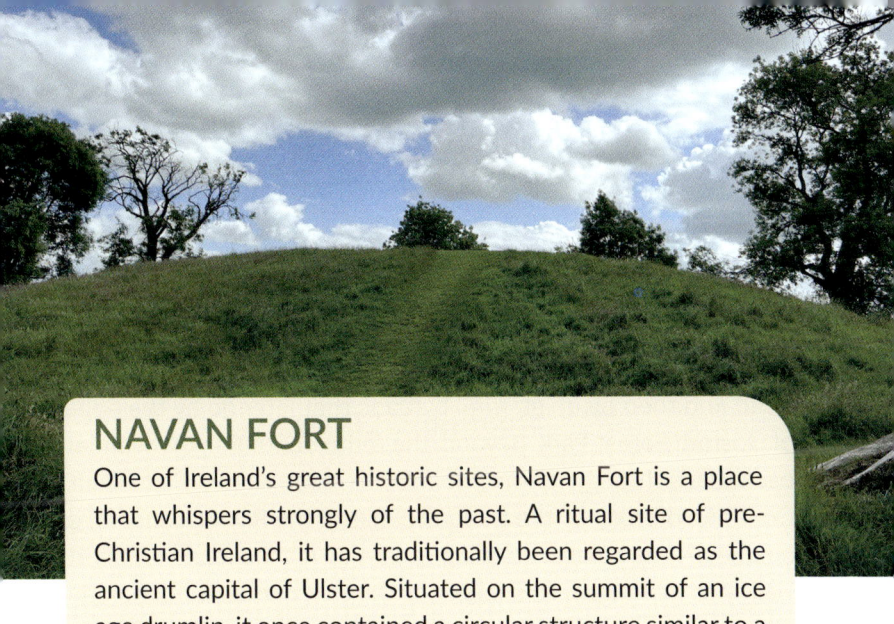

NAVAN FORT

One of Ireland's great historic sites, Navan Fort is a place that whispers strongly of the past. A ritual site of pre-Christian Ireland, it has traditionally been regarded as the ancient capital of Ulster. Situated on the summit of an ice age drumlin, it once contained a circular structure similar to a temple, which, for some unexplained reason, was destroyed by fire. In Irish mythology, Navan Fort is the royal capital of the Ulaidh race; these were the ancient people who gave their name to the province of Ulster. At one time the Fort was reputed to have been the residence of Conchobar mac Nessa, king of Ulster. He is said to have had a warrior school here for his royal soldiers who were titled the Red Branch Knights.

Ireland's religious capital. You will discover that Armagh, the last resting place of renowned Irish High King, Brian Ború, is one of Ireland's hidden gems. If you visit both the Catholic and Church of Ireland cathedrals, which are located on hilltops, you will most certainly be captivated by the breathtaking views over the city. Armagh is the seat of the Primate of All Ireland for both the Roman Catholic and the Church of Ireland communities. The city is rich in elegant architecture and fascinating Christian heritage, offering a tree-lined mall, Georgian streets and many heritage sites.

DAY 2

ARMAGH TO TANDRAGEE
25KM

Leaving Armagh City by way of the busy A28 Markethill Road, you enjoy the benefit of a footpath before swinging left onto Edenaveys Road. Afterwards, it is right onto Ballynahonemore Road and then by quiet, rural byroads that later go by the edge of Gosford Forest Park. Beyond, the route continues to meander back roads through farming country to reach scenic Clare Glen. Continue off-road by the tranquil banks of the River Cusher for a couple of kms before returning to tarmac for the relatively short walk into Tandragee. This was once the seat of the Irish O'Hanlon clan until their lands were confiscated in the early 16th century as part of the Ulster Plantation.

DAY 3
TANDRAGEE TO NEWRY
25KM

This morning it is asphalt all the way to reach the now-disused Ulster Canal. Here, the route swings south along the Newry section of the canal towpath leading to Scarva Village, which is renowned for its floral displays in summer. Beyond, St Patrick's Way continues to follow the Newry towpath on a relatively level surface. Here, you are walking beside the oldest summit-level canal in Britain and Ireland, which means that the canal moves, not downhill, but uphill and must, therefore, have a water supply. Below Scarva, the route passes scenic Lough Shark, which was the feeder lake supplying water to the highest sections of the canal. Then it is on by the substantial town of Poyntzpass, where services are available, before continuing on a pleasant but uneventful 14km waterside walk to reach Newry.

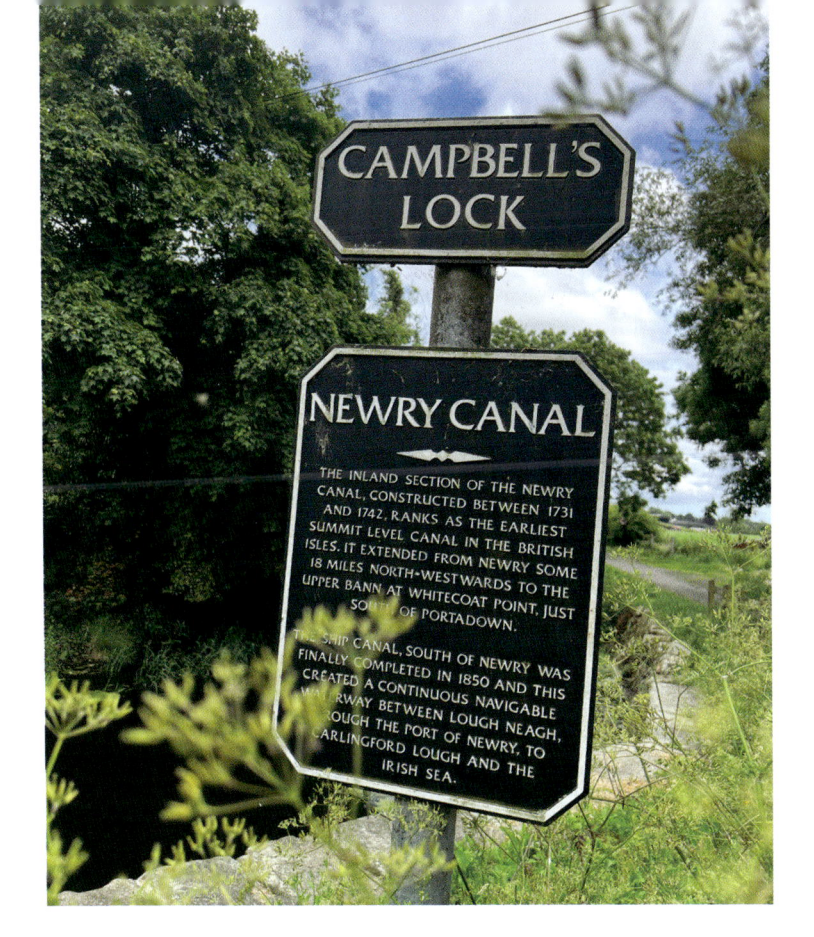

With a population today of over 27,000, Newry was founded in 1157 by Cistercian monks who were newly arrived to Ireland. In the 16th century, the abbey was dissolved during the Reformation and the English stronghold of Bagenal's Castle was built on the Abbey site. Newry is now an important market town and is the episcopal seat of the Roman Catholic Diocese of Dromore. In 2002, along with Lisburn, it was granted city status. The stamping point for your passport is on an external wall outside the Town Hall.

DAY 4

NEWRY TO ROSTREVOR
15KM

Leave Newry by ascending Courtney Hill and continue along Ballyholland Road. Soon the way meanders through a maze of quiet back roads to pass north of pretty Greenan Lough to the East of Milltown Lough. The route then begins its descent towards Carlingford Lough offering stunning scenery across the water to the historic Cooley Mountains, which are located in the Irish Republic. To your left, the mighty Mourne Mountains fill the horizon as you approach the pretty Edwardian village of Rostrevor. Since today was a relatively short outing, you should have time to visit the delightful Rostrevor Beach which faces south. It is a nice place to catch some rays of the evening sun, if the weather obliges.

DAY 5

ROSTREVOR TO SPELGA PASS
18KM

This section of the route begins your traverse through the foothills of the Mourne Mountains and will eventually lead to Newcastle – an attractive resort on the Irish Sea. Starting in Rostrevor, it is immediately uphill along forest paths in Kilbroney Forest Park and Rostrevor Forest. Next comes open mountainside, with the path continuing roughly north and paralleling the Rostrevor to Hilltown Road, which lies to the left.

Swinging right, the Way ascends steeply uphill around Rocky Mountain to reach a well-surfaced mountain track known as the New Bog Road. Go left here. After about 2km swing right around the slopes of Hen Mountain following a wall. Leaving the wall, tag the arrows to a footbridge over the infant River Bann and continue uphill to reach the B27 Kilkeel Road, which marks the end of your day's outing. If you do not intend to camp wild, you will need to arrange a pick-up from this point and a return the following morning.

DAY 6

SPELGA PASS TO NEWCASTLE
19KM

This morning you have a choice. You can strike out over open mountainside with a steep climb to gain the summits of Butter Mountain and Slievenamuck where navigation skills will be required in poor weather. Alternately, you can stay on the asphalt by going right for about 2.5km, with the waters of the Spelga Reservoir below until you reach a T-Junction. Go left here and continue for about 1.5km where the route turns right and leads along the eastern shore of Fofanny Reservoir. Continue along the path beneath the slopes of Slieve Meelbeg to reach a stone wall. Go right on a path beside the wall leading east to join the Trassey Track, which was originally part of a smuggling route through the Mournes for illicit liquor coming ashore from the Irish Sea.

Follow this track left to a public road. Almost immediately go right into Tollymore Forest Park and track the pretty Shimna River past Kings Grave and Parnell Bridge before going right to reach the southern edge of Tollymore where you exit the Park. Trail the signs along a lane and a public road. Now enter Tipperary Wood and follow the walking arrows to reach Newcastle and then the Tourist Information Centre on the Promenade at the town centre.

DAY 7
NEWCASTLE TO BALLYKINLER
17KM

Start today by rambling along the town Promenade to the Slieve Donard Hotel. Continue following the beach north for about 3km with the world-famous Royal County Down Golf Club on your left. Ascend from the beach and tag a wooden boardwalk through the dunes of Murlough Bay Nature Reserve. Go right and immediately right again to a lane leading for about 2.5km to the southern end of Dundrum and then continue through the centre of the village. From the National Trust car park to the north of Dundrum, the coastal path runs along a disused railway line that once connected Belfast and Newcastle. This serene trail takes you by a delightful grassy corridor, offering trees to your left and coastal views on your right with a causeway at one stage having water on the 2 sides. Here you are likely to spot wading birds standing motionless on the mudflats while searching for the relatively abundant food supply.

Leave the old railway line by descending steps and continuing to a minor road which leads to the A2 Blackstaff Road. Here, a right turn takes you over Blackstaff Bridge. In less than a 1km, continue straight ahead along Ford Road and then Commons Road for a total of about 3km to reach Ballykinler village which became well known during the Irish War of Independence as an internment camp for republican prisoners.

DAY 8

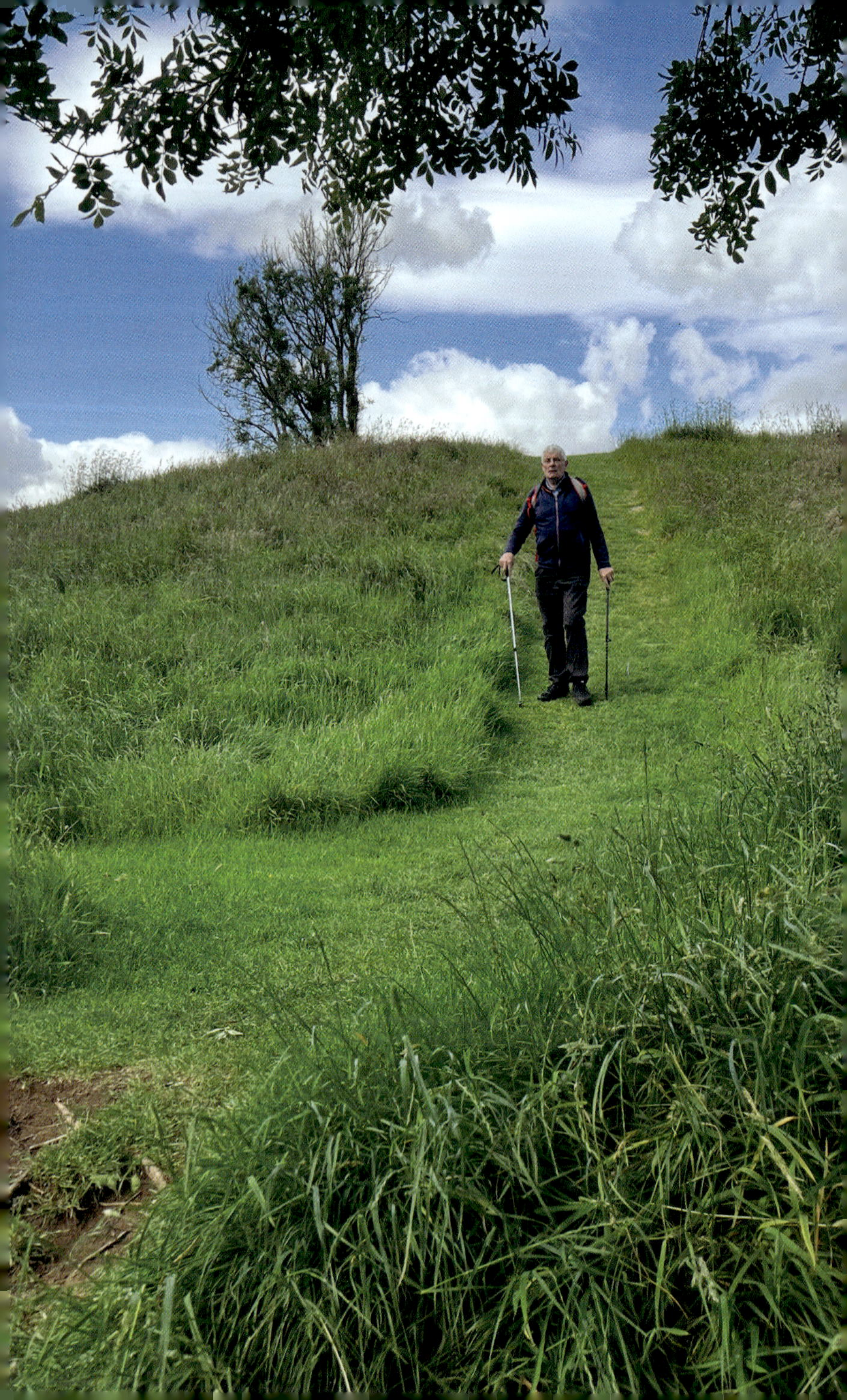

BALLYKINLER TO DOWNPATRICK
17KM

Today, you reach the end of the journey at Downpatrick. It is in the vicinity of this town that Patrick's Irish mission is reputed to have begun and finally ended. After the wonderful 2-day crossing of the Mourne Mountains and yesterday's memorable coastal walk, today may, however, seem an anti-climax. Your final day is entirely on tarmac and takes serene but rather mundane back roads while passing only one tiny hamlet, that of Ballynoe. Your approach to Downpatrick is along the A25 and then up Market Street. To the left is the modern and stylish St Patrick's Centre where you end your pilgrim journey and receive the final stamp if you are filling a pilgrim passport. The Centre has a well-laid-out visitor experience telling the story of the Saint's life and is the world's only permanent exhibition dedicated to St Patrick.

Afterwards, it would be remiss not to walk the short distance up the hill from behind St Patrick's Centre to visit Down Church of Ireland Cathedral. This was built as a Benedictine monastery in the late 12th century when the Normans were introducing European orders of monks to Ireland and is located on the site of a much earlier monastic settlement. The Cathedral, which is free to visit, contains magnificent stained-glass windows, but the main attraction lies in the cathedral grounds. An inscribed stone of Mourne granite marks the reputed final resting place of St Patrick, who died in the year 461, following a 29-year evangelical mission in Ireland.

◀ Author John G O'Dwyer on St Patrick's Way

Acknowledgements

To the members of the Mid-Tipp Hillwalkers club who stoically endured my company for over 30 years of exploring in all corners of Ireland and were my valued companions on many of the walks described.

To the landowners of Ireland who continue, despite many reports to the contrary, to provide unhindered access to the vast majority of our upland and wilderness areas.

To Diarmaid Condon, Grainne Moynihan and Conor Ryan for their assistance.

A special word of thanks to Garry O'Sullivan of Currach Books for placing his trust in my endeavour, book designer Alba Esteban and Paula Nolan for her persistence and dedication in giving shape to this book.

To Jim McNicholas of the Irish Camino Society for his help with the Celtic Camino chapters.

Finally, to my wife Carmel for her advice and patience in correcting my errors and omissions and countless hours spent in finishing the script.

While acknowledging the contribution of all the above – any remaining errors or omissions are entirely my responsibility.

WOULD YOU LIKE TO READ MORE?

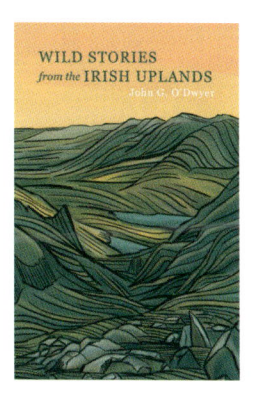

In *Wild Stories from the Irish Uplands*, veteran hiker John G. O'Dwyer draws upon his treasure trove of experience to recount captivating tales of the Irish uplands from times gone by – from saints and scoundrels, to rescuers, rebels and rapparees. He seamlessly merges expert historical sources with his own fact-finding walks through the uplands to create a vivid picture of Ireland's past. The book successfully relates how Ireland's vertically unassuming mountains and hills have been central to the ebb and flow of Irish life for countless generations, with accounts of these events woven afterwards into unifying local mythologies.

ISBN 9781782189121 | Paperback | 196 pp

www.currachbooks.com

WOULD YOU LIKE TO READ MORE?

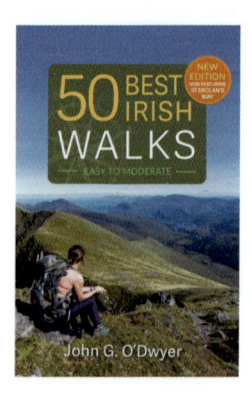

50 BEST IRISH WALKS
John G. O'Dwyer

John G. O'Dwyer's Irish walks have become famous through his column in The Irish Times. Now his 50 favorite rambles are gathered here in one pocket-sized volume.

A must read for anyone interested in Ireland's hills and mountains, these trails range from easy to moderate walks all around Ireland, taking anywhere from 1.5 to 4.5 hours to complete. Accompanied by beautiful photographs of the stunning Irish landscape, this is an ideal collection for the avid walker.

ISBN 9781782189350 | Paperback | 240 pp

www.currachbooks.com